"Not For A Million Dollars"

The cult demanded all —
her mind, her body, her children —
until the day
she said . . .

"Not For A Million Dollars"

Una McManus
and
John Charles Cooper

impact
books

Nashville, Tennessee

The authors and publisher wish to express their appreciation to the following publishers for permission to quote from the following copyrighted materials:

Reflections, Paul Tournier. Copyright © 1976 by Harper & Row, SCM Press Limited. Used by permission.

"Beware—'The Children of God,'" Kenneth P. Frampton. Used by permission.

All Scripture quotations are from The King James Version of the Bible.

Library of Congress Catalog Card Number: 80–81754

ISBN 0–914850–54-7

M0554

*To John and Michael
hoping someday they'll understand.*

Table of Contents

Preface

The other day my best friend made a comment that aptly describes what I want to say about my story: "You know, you can kill a man with the Bible by hitting him over the head with it."

Although I suffered many things at the hands of people who claimed to be Christians, I do not blame the Church or refute Christian beliefs. Rather, I am attempting to show how these Christian truths were distorted by wolves in the cult's clothing and used to further their own devious ends of enslaving and exploiting sincere young people.

By telling my sometimes painful story I hope that I may accomplish two objectives: first, to illustrate the acute need for young people to be well-informed about cults and aware of the danger posed by their subtle distortion of religious truths, so they will not be led, as I was, a dumb sheep to the slaughter.

Secondly, to urge society, particularly the religious, to be more aware, sympathetic and helpful toward ex-cult victims. The road back is long and hard and we all need help to make it. We joined because we wanted to serve God and better our world. We were guilty only of being in the wrong place at the wrong time, where our sincere religious beliefs were perverted by deceivers.

Una McManus
Akron, Ohio

The Judgment

The judge looked down at me, compassion softening his stern features.

"Get ready," my attorney, Mrs. Leda Hartwell, whispered.

Beginning softly, his voice rising with emotion, Judge William Gillie of the Franklin County Court of Common Pleas intoned, "Frankly, young lady, I've been appalled by this case. I've heard few stories in this courtroom to equal it. It's shocking that religion can become so twisted that even the lives of little children are endangered. How could religious teachings become so perverted that immorality is considered a sacred duty? Obviously, money can't recompense you for the physical and emotional damages done. How can I put a price on your experience?" Judge Gillie glanced at me kindly. "Mrs. Hartwell, do you have a sum in mind?"

Mrs. Hartwell was flustered for a moment. She looked at me, her eyes unfocused. My attorney knew that money was not what I was after, but the exposure of those who misuse the spiritual longings of the young. After consulting some papers on the table, she rose and spoke confidently.

"Your Honor, the plaintiff feels that not even a million dollars would compensate her for the suffering of the past five years."

Judge Gillie pondered, then punctuated his decision with one emphatic whack of the gavel. "This court awards Una McManus one million dollars in compensatory damages and one-half million dollars in punitive damages against the Children of God religious cult and its leader, David Brandt Berg, also known as Moses David, for alienation of her husband's affection and for the misrepresentation of their ideals."

I was stunned. After all these years of abuse and exploitation, I was vindicated. The Children of God were culpable, guilty, at fault for leading me astray.

Judge Gillie had brought my seven-year quest for freedom from fear and for acceptance as a wronged truth-seeker to an end.

The judge left the courtroom. I turned to thank Mrs. Hartwell.

"Well, that's your second court victory," she observed. "You've already won the custody of your sons. John-John and Michael are yours to raise in a normal manner."

"Yes," I answered. "Thanks to you and Mr. Hewitt."

Before I could say anything more, my best friend, Marcia Carroll, approached from the spectators' seats.

"Well, Una, congratulations!" Marcia cried. "You won. We all won. Everyone who fights the cults won today!" Marcia's grin was spread all over her face.

Marcia, too, was an ex-cultist. Now she often served as a deprogrammer with Ted Patrick, the famous (or infamous) man who first recognized the mind control practiced by the cultists and set out to combat it.

Thank the dear Lord, it's all over, I thought gratefully.

How did I ever become involved in anything so bizarre? Only a few years ago, I was a fifteen-year-old hippie kid, estranged from the Catholic Church, seeking freedom from my parents, flirting with drugs in my native Dublin, in Ireland, the isle of saints and scholars . . .

1
Is It All Worthwhile?

I have always been sensitive to spiritual things. Even my birthday, coming two days before Christmas, had religious significance for me. I lived with my parents and my older sister, Pervaneh, in a typical Irish Catholic home. Pervaneh and I, like many others in that country, were baptized in infancy and educated by nuns.

As a young child, encouraged particularly by my grandmother, I was unusually devout. Perhaps I fancied myself a young Saint Joan, waiting to hear the "voices" that would determine my destiny. Nevertheless, at the age of nine, I rose very early, before the rest of the family, and attended daily Mass. Breaks in school sometimes found me praying my rosary, fingering the beads hidden in my pocket, while my companions clowned around. At home I decorated my bedroom with religious emblems which I bought out of my own pocket money. When I was ten my father and mother decided to send me to the convent boarding school where my sister was educated. I was delighted, as I had always wanted to become a nun.

But life in boarding school was filled with loneliness and unwelcome restrictions. We girls formed attachments among ourselves, clinging to each other for security and warmth in the impersonal atmosphere. We defied the musty traditions by smoking cigarettes in the restrooms and sneaking off the grounds for afternoons of fun in the town.

It was in this way that news of the drug culture reached our cloistered world. Always adventurous, I felt compelled to explore this forbidden territory. I knew nothing at all about drugs, but I was curious.

Armed with a few Irish pounds and a determination to find out what it was all about, I wandered around the grounds of Trinity College in Dublin and met Jeffrey, a small, dapper student from England. Jeffrey was amused by my candor when I asked if he could sell me some drugs, but led me down to the student café. There, under the dim lights and among the tables crowded with Bohemian-looking students, he told me the facts of life about street drugs. I learned there were drugs to swallow and drugs to smoke. He explained the variety of highs that accompanied the different drugs. The afternoon wore on and I listened enthralled.

When his friends finally came, they sold me one square inch of hashish wrapped in aluminum foil. I fingered the package in my pocket, savoring the pride and thrill of possessing a ticket to the sophisticated life-styles that surrounded me. In this way I was introduced to the drug subculture.

By the time I was fifteen, I was dabbling in LSD as well as hashish. I had also transferred to a day school and had a Saturday job in a hippie boutique in the heart of Dublin.

I was working in the boutique one Saturday when a few of my hippie friends came in to visit me. We took some LSD together. My friends told me about some strange people they had met in the park that afternoon.

"They don't work for money," someone said. "They just travel around talking about God."

"How irresponsible," I shrugged with contempt. "They should earn their own living, not leech off society."

Then the LSD began to take effect and I lost all consciousness of time. I felt giddy and light-headed and laughed aloud when someone tried to steal a dress. Again that day, I sold nothing, to my boss's mounting displeasure.

After work I went with my friends to smoke a joint in the park before dinner. Crossing the four-lane street to the park posed problems. In my drugged state the cars became animated and their grilles leered and snarled at me. Nagging fears set in. As I walked behind my friends through the park, I eyed everyone suspiciously. Behind every trench coat and second glance, I saw a plainclothes detective waiting to arrest me. I reached our rendezvous point as the others were passing around the first joint. I took one long drag and grew panicky.

"I've got to get out of here," I announced to my happy, "high" friends. "I'm being watched by the fuzz."

After hurrying away from the others, I sauntered along beside the lake, savoring the peaceful stillness of the water. Glancing toward the benches that lined the path, I spotted two disheveled hippies. Judging from their Bibles and guitars, I supposed them to be the Jesus people I'd heard about earlier. Hoping to avoid them, I looked in the other direction as I passed their bench and pretended to be absorbed in the reflections of the late afternoon sun on the water.

Ah, made it without being stopped, I sighed.

Too soon.

Behind me I heard the sound of running footsteps and a man's voice with an unmistakable American accent calling after me.

"Hey, stop! Are you a lost sheep? Stop! Stop!"

Embarrassed, and hoping to avoid conversation, I answered,

"No, I'm not a lost sheep."

He caught up with me, panting breathlessly and waving his guitar in the air. "Hi! I'm Steven," he grinned.

"Hi," I said, thinking, *What a weird character*!

"Hey, you *look* like a lost sheep. Come and sit with us."

More than anything else, I wanted to get away.

"No, no, I must go," I pleaded. His intense gaze was hard to break. I could see he wasn't playing games. He was intent on persuading me to come and sit on the bench with him and his companion. *Why was it so important to him that I come and talk to him?* I wondered. Why, that was it! Yes, he and his lady friend were plainclothes members of the drug squad. I had heard horror stories about policemen and women who donned hippie garb and mingled with the hippies, seeking to arrest the unwary drug user. So that was what they wanted! Behind their innocent grins I could see their true motive. They weren't fooling me at all. I was going to outsmart them. I'd play along with their little game. I'd sit on their bench and talk to them. I'd act straight as a poker and they would never suspect that I was high.

I followed the young man to the wooden bench several yards back down the path. I sat down between him and the short, plump woman whom he introduced as his wife, Rejoice. Then Steven proceeded to tell me about Jesus.

He glowed as he told me of his experience. "Meeting and knowing God is so simple," he insisted. "All you have to do to be saved is to pray, asking Jesus to come into your heart." This idea was new to me.

Rejoice now entered the conversation enthusiastically. Glassy-eyed to the point that I thought she, too, was high on drugs, she told me of her wonderful life now that she had found God and His Son, Jesus Christ.

Somewhere along the line I abandoned the idea that these people were plainclothes detectives. Now, no longer compelled by fear to listen, I listened to them out of curiosity. I thought I'd never met such beautiful people. They seemed so happy and sincere, so utterly without hatred or strife. Warm, loving vibrations flowed between them. I sensed they were concerned about me and wanted to extend these warm vibes to me also. So I stayed, and I listened. An hour went by. I was entranced by their reference to the family they belonged to, and wanted to hear more.

My friends came looking for me and tried to drag me away.

"Don't waste your time with these Jesus freaks," begged my friend Debbie, who was tugging on my sleeve.

"No, leave me alone. I want to hear what these people have to say."

My friends left in disgust, but I hardly noticed. Steven played his guitar and sang me a happy little song describing how one must become "a baby to go to heaven." His childlike faith was captivating. Listening to him, his agile body swaying in time to his music, the answers to life seemed so simple. I too could be happy and fulfilled, Steven promised. He gave me a pamphlet that would show me how.

"I think she's a lost sheep," Steven grinned at Rejoice.

"Yes," replied Rejoice, smiling warmly at me. "You're one of Jesus' lost sheep and we're here to lead you to His true fold. Would you like to pray with us and receive Him into your heart? Then you can go to Heaven when you die."

Unaccustomed to praying aloud in public places, I was embarrassed by her offer and declined.

"Oh, but you must pray with us. You don't want to go to hell, do you?" Rejoice persisted.

"No, but I won't pray with you now," I insisted. "Maybe later."

"We'll pray for you," smiled Rejoice, squeezing my hand.

Again, I was impressed by the warmth and sincerity of these strange foreigners. Not even my closest friends showered me with so much attention. Their urgent concern for me and my soul touched me. I felt wanted and believed they cared for me.

"If you won't pray with us, at least come and visit us," Rejoice said as we parted at the park gate. "Our address is on the back of the pamphlet. Remember—we love you."

2
The Children of God

A week later, while cleaning out my purse, I found the pamphlet Steven had given me. Out of curiosity, I reread it and even prayed the prayer outlined on the back. It was a simple prayer, asking God for forgiveness of sins and receiving Jesus as my Savior. I remembered the love and sincerity I had seen in the faces of the two Jesus people and decided to keep my promise to visit them.

I knocked tentatively on the door. I wasn't prepared for the handsome, young bearded man who answered my knock. He invited me in and called for Steven and Rejoice. As I stepped into the narrow hallway, many people tumbled down the stairs and hung over the rail chorusing, "Hi!"; "We love you!"; and "Praise the Lord!" Stunned by this display of friendliness, I was led into the living room. At one end of the room was a fireplace, and the only furniture was a rickety wooden stand containing some literature.

Rejoice came bounding in. Her enthusiasm and zest were electrifying.

"We are so glad you came!" she exclaimed in a voice pitched high with excitement. "We love you!"

I was flattered to be welcomed so warmly by someone I barely knew. Rejoice began to make light conversation asking how I had been, where I lived, and the size of my family. She soon got around to asking, "Did you read the pamphlet we gave you?"

"Yes, I did."

"Did you ask Jesus to come into your heart?"

"Yes, I did."

I was startled by her reaction. "Hallelujah!" she shouted, jumping up and down and clapping her hands. She informed me that all the angels in heaven were rejoicing because my soul was saved. I was taken aback by her display of emotion but felt pleased that my soul merited such attention. Rejoice ran excitedly into the hall and told five or six others who joined in ecstatic praise. I was welcomed into their circle. Mystified by the importance of repeating a simple prayer but, enjoying this attention, I went right along with the game. It was easy to pretend I understood the significance of what I had done.

Soon Magdala, from Margate, England, sat down on the floor beside me. She called me "Sister." Together, we leafed through a large photo album—page after page of smiling faces. These were pictures of Family members. The "Family" referred collectively to all the people living in the house, or "colony," she explained.

"We are all brothers and sisters here," Magdala said. "And members of the Family take biblical names to symbolize their new life in Christ." In time my name was changed to "Melita," the name used for the island of Malta in the book of Acts.

As I listened, there was a constant passage of people through the hallway and up the stairs. The majority were young men—ages sixteen to twenty-four, some of whom were American. People shouted back and forth. "Well, praise the Lord, Brother!" "I love you!" "Jesus loves you." Kisses and hugs were exchanged. The atmosphere vibrated with joy.

Steven sat on the floor beside me, expressing delight

at what he termed my acceptance of Christ. Looking me straight in the eye, he told me of God's love for me and His plan for those faithful few who devote their lives to serving Him.

Again I heard Magdala's message: "We are God's Family and we live together as brothers and sisters. We live our lives only to serve the Lord. Our Family lives in peace, love, and joy while the rest of the world suffers the effects of hate and violence."

I could certainly relate to hatred and violence. Those elements were very much a part of life in Ireland—the troubles in the North; the terrorists; the gangs of short-haired thugs who roamed the streets at night beating up people. Steven went on to say that none of the commune members worked at secular jobs but spent their days "serving the Lord and spreading the Gospel." For the second time in recent weeks, I balked.

"Why, that's sheer irresponsibility," I said indignantly.

"No, not at all," replied Steven quickly and defensively, his voice edged with impatience. "Our work is spreading the Gospel. It's God's work. He provides for us."

I retorted, "What if everybody were to stop working and lived like this? How would we all then survive?"

"Well," replied Steven confidently, "very few people love God enough to do that."

That was it, straight and simple. I had no comeback.

The room filled for the evening meal. Rejoice invited me to eat with them. I accepted eagerly and telephoned my mother. She was wary. "Una, who are these people?" she asked. I replied by describing the happy group of Christian young people I'd met.

When I returned, all twenty-five Family members were singing a simple grace: "Thank you, Jesus, for this food." Their voices rang with sincerity.

It was a hot summer evening, so we took our plates

outside. The food was plain but the company was good. Congenial groups sat together on the grass, eating and talking. The girls were pretty. Was it because of their happy smiles? The young men were attractive, bearded, and wore their hair fashionably long. A number of them came to embrace me as we finished our meal.

After the meal, everyone crowded into the living room for the evening get-together. While a few of the boys tuned their guitars, Rejoice and I chatted by the fireplace. I mentioned that I was a Roman Catholic. She expressed disapproval, and I responded with one of the few Catholic doctrines I remembered from Catechism class:

"But didn't Jesus say to Peter, 'Thou art Peter, and upon this rock I will build my church; . . . and I will give unto thee the keys of the kingdom of heaven' (Matt. 16:18–19)?"

Rejoice immediately seized upon this verse and quoted other Scripture from the Bible to substantiate her claim that it was Jesus, not Peter, upon whom the Church was built. I wasn't convinced, but I was silenced. I wasn't too concerned; I hadn't been to church for some time.

The singing and clapping began. The people stood in a circle and, led by the guitar players, sang spirited religious songs that told of their love for God and their desire to serve Him. The atmosphere in the room became emotionally charged. Members of the Family flung their arms into the air and shouted praises to God, sometimes speaking in an unintelligible language. As the session wore on, people grew more and more ecstatic, reaching a peak comparable to a drug-induced high.

At ten o'clock Steven announced that it was time to wind up so the Family members could retire. At his word the group broke up. Several members came over to wish me good night.

As I was ushered to the door, someone pressed a

small book into my hand. It was the Gospel of John. Feeling emotionally high after the inspiration session, I was overjoyed to think I held in my hand the answers to all the problems of the world. As Steven waved from the door, I called back to him:

"Hey, what's the name of your group, anyhow?"

"We are called the Children of God."

3
New Life — —
And Death

I was drawn again and again to that little house. I didn't understand all the purposes of the group or how it functioned. All I knew was that it felt good to be around these friendly people who loved me just as I was. At fifteen, struggling through adolescence, it felt *very* good.

Rejoice invited me to attend Bible classes. Since school was out for the summer, I visited the Family every day. During the "classes," Rejoice used passages of Scripture to explain the Family's beliefs and practices.

"Jesus called His disciples to follow Him, give up all their worldly goods, and live communally—just like we do," she spoke convincingly. "The Bible says that if a man does not forsake all that he has, he cannot be Christ's disciple.

"You're wasting your time going to school and preparing to get a job, Una, because the Bible says you can't serve God and mammon. The prophet Hosea says that he who earns wages earns them to fill a pocket full of holes. Come, and do God's will . . . join us."

In the next six months, that invitation became a living, beckoning thing. In an all-out battle for my soul, the brothers and sisters joined forces against the "system"—society outside the Family, which they considered to be the domain of the Devil.

One Saturday I walked to the shop to begin work. My employer met me at the door. "I won't be needing you anymore, Una," she said.

"What's that?" I asked.

"Why, I don't need you today—nor any Saturday for the rest of the summer," she replied.

"Did I do something wrong?" I asked in a tight voice.

"Dear," she said sharply, "you just can't sell."

My image of myself as a "with-it" hippie saleslady was shattered. I was hurt, and angry at the shop owner.

When I visited the Family that afternoon, Rejoice insisted that nothing happens without a purpose. God was speaking to me through every event. Losing my job, according to Rejoice, was God's sign that I should give up the world and join the Family.

Before meeting the Family, I was a fun-loving daredevil. Now, belligerently, I tried to convert my classmates.

Sorcha Malone, one of my best friends, asked me one day, "Una, why do you always have your nose stuck in the Bible? What's so interesting about it?"

"Well, Sorcha, I've found God and the true way to serve Him. Nothing else matters anymore."

I showed her Scriptures that the Family had taught me. She decided that she, too, was going to read the Bible, beginning with the very first chapter. She read as far as the story of Cain and Abel before she grew disillusioned.

"I can't understand why God was mad at Cain's offering, but pleased with Abel's. That seems unfair to me. I don't know if I want anything to do with such a whimsical God."

I, of course, had no explanation, so Sorcha gave up reading the Bible and a potential convert slipped through my fingers.

That night I asked Steven about the passage. He confidently answered, "God was displeased with Cain's offering because he was on a works trip. He worked to till the land to produce the food he offered to God and, therefore, he felt he had earned his salvation. Cain, on the other hand, simply relied on God's mercy and had faith. That's why God was pleased with him. People in churches today are all trying to earn their salvation through their good works, and God is angry with them. But He's pleased with us because we live by faith, trusting Him to provide for us."

I got the message loud and clear: the Children of God were better than the churches.

As my sixteenth birthday drew near, I pleaded with my parents to let me join the Family, telling them they were wasting their money sending me to school. I threatened to run away and join the Children of God if they didn't give their permission. And even if I didn't run away, I'd still join as soon as I was of legal age.

I felt very angry at my parents and sister—and angry at my other relatives as well. I felt that I did not belong there. I was being held prisoner against my will—a prisoner kept from God's plan for my life and my personal independence.

Nothing my mother or father said changed my thinking or feelings a bit. I wouldn't accept my father's logical rebuttals of the Family's claims. When Mother pointed out to me that the Scriptures I proclaimed might be quoted out of context and even misinterpreted, I refused to acknowledge what she said.

My sister, I just ignored.

To drown out the voices of love and reason, I ranted on and on at the top of my voice, "The System is corrupt. The Church is perverted. If you are part of the System and the Church, then you are corrupt and perverted, too."

When my family looked at me in shocked surprise, I simply glared back in smug self-righteousness.

If anyone were ever alienated—self-alienated—from their loved ones—I was.

Finally on December 1, twenty-two days before my birthday, my father gave in. He felt that joining the Family was something I needed to get out of my system and that I'd be home within a few weeks. Gaining their permission was a real victory from the Lord, I believed. Gleefully, I packed my bags and prepared to move in with the Family.

When I called my friend, Debbie, to say goodbye, I was met with silence, except for muffled sobs.

"Debbie, are you there? Is something the matter?"

"Haven't you heard what happened to Sorcha?"

Oh, no, I thought, *she must have gotten caught staying out late*.

"No, I haven't. What's the matter with Sorcha?"

"She's . . . dead."

"You're joking!"

"No, I'm not. I wouldn't joke about a thing like that."

Sorcha couldn't be dead. Not our lively, laughing Sorcha! Why, I'd seen her only two days earlier. The room seemed to withdraw, leaving me alone in empty space. My stomach turned over. My head began to spin.

Sorcha's death was the end of the world for me—not figuratively, but literally. If I had any lingering doubts about breaking away from home, any fears about life in the Family, they dissolved in the hot tears that poured down my cheeks. Sorcha died in the System's world—in a System way, by an automobile. Her death killed something in me, too. I decisively broke with the System—the world of my mother and father, family, school and church—at least for that time and for a long time to come.

I packed a few clothes and, carrying my one valuable possession, a sewing machine, I left home and went to join my new Family. They would help me.

Once at the house I poured out my story. A brother

chided me, "Don't be so despondent. You ought to be happy when someone goes to be with the Lord." Obediently, I suppressed my grief and threw myself vigorously into my new life.

4

Babes
in the
Wilderness

December of 1972 was bitterly cold. The Family was living in a drafty old mansion by Dublin Bay, provided by a policeman sympathetic to our cause. It was in bad repair, but the Family worked hard to make it livable. Broken windows were replaced; pipe and sewer lines were relaid; the gas lines were reconnected, and inside walls were painted with materials supplied by interested businessmen in the community.

Several members were made "provisioners," and they visited merchants in the city to solicit material and financial help. These businessmen were persuaded that they were contributing to a Christian drug-rehabilitation center. The truth was that while many members had been involved with drug use, they were required to abandon the habit upon joining the Family and no concentrated effort was ever made to help cure hard-core drug addicts. In fact, during my first few months in the Family, our leaders instructed us not to "waste time" on drug addicts "since they are too hard to train."

And training was what it was all about. A new convert was known as a "babe" until he had completed his basic training program. This program consisted of a rigorous schedule of Bible classes; teachings of the founder, Moses David; and memorization, generally lasting three to six months. At that point the babe became an "older brother or sister" and, at the discretion of the colony shepherd, could teach classes and lead in the morning devotions. After three more months he became a "Leader in Training." At this stage he was given more responsibility and, if he proved loyal, was admitted to the coveted "leadership sessions" which were held late at night. During these sessions, colony policy was discussed, decisions were made, and confidential Moses David letters were read. These letters provided the real meat of the Children of God's plans and teachings and only the leaders were allowed access to them.

The sexes were strictly segregated regarding sleeping arrangements. The single males slept on the second floor and the sisters on the third. The two married couples had their own rooms in a separate wing. No dating or sexual contact was allowed among the unmarried members, and marriage was permitted only for members who had proved their loyalty and spent six months to a year with the Family. The girls wore no makeup and they donned long, shapeless gowns lest they arouse lust in their brothers.

The babes arose at six o'clock and had a brief half hour for washing up (in cold water), dressing, prayer and memorizing. Each new member was given a "set-card." On this little card were printed ten groups of biblical references. Each group or set listed ten or twelve verses which were to be memorized. These verses had been selected by a leader of the Family and served to reinforce the teachings. Sets One and Two contained simple, fundamental verses about Jesus Christ and salvation—verses that average churchgoers would know.

Later sets listed more controversial material. Scriptures that could be easily misinterpreted were taken out of context, sometimes with disastrous results. One example is Matthew 10:36–38 and Luke 14:26: "And a man's foes shall be they of his own household. He that loveth father or mother more than me is not worthy of me: and he that loveth son or daughter more than me is not worthy of me. And he that taketh not his cross, and followeth after me, is not worthy of me. If any man come to me, and hate not his father, and mother, and wife, and children, and brethren, and sisters, yea, and his own life also, he cannot be my disciple." The Family used these verses to teach rejection of parents or relatives who did not agree with their doctrines. Hostile parents were known inside the group as "Matthew 10:36'ers," and their children were sometimes moved to a secret locality. Of course, this action was justifiable because the parents were said to be acting under the influence of Satan.

We learned that the Family's definition of God's love was used to justify just about anything. The love of God necessitated our leaving home over the protests of parents or spouses. God's love required us to serve Him one hundred percent with the Family, denouncing education and secular jobs as evil symbols of Devil worship. God's love would ultimately judge the wickedness of the world system. Apparently, only the Children of God would escape judgment. Strangely enough, God's love was also used to keep us in subjection. God loved us so much that, if we strayed from the Family, he would punish us, perhaps through sickness or death, or by allowing us to be tormented by the Devil. At the very least, we would certainly lose our heavenly rewards. We were to submit ourselves body and soul to our leaders. Implicit obedience and belief without question were demanded and received. I was taught that if my leader told me to do something wrong, I was to obey, as if God Himself had spoken, and I would not be held accountable. Doubts about the teachings were the voice of the Devil and were to be suppressed.

Prophetic Scriptures were used to prove that the end

of the world was near and that God was going to destroy the capitalistic West and the Church through the
Communists.

One evening while we were sitting in a circle on the
floor, one leader burst in the door, shouting wildly and
waving a toy machine gun. He pointed it at us and pretended to spray the room with gunfire. "Rat-at-at! Rat-
at-at!" For a moment I believed it was for real; the end
had come.

"Ha! How many of you guys were really prepared?"
taunted the leader. "It's going to happen just that
quickly. Don't ever forget that for one minute. We can
expect to be persecuted for our faith. We'd better be
ready to be captured, tortured, or even killed. But, if
we're faithful, we'll stand with the Lamb. Hallelujah!"

After several hours of indoctrination, we ate a snack
and hitched or walked into town to try out our newly-
learned proselytizing skills. We were instructed to aim
for lost-looking hippies. Travelers were particularly
good targets.

After approaching a likely-looking individual, we
started a friendly conversation. We steered the conversation to religion as soon as possible and presented ar-
guments as to why this person should receive Christ. If
we persuaded him on these points, we moved in to
invite him to join the Family. Often, we invited the
"sheep" home for dinner and fellowship, thus buying
more time to work on the person.

Everyone made a special effort to make visitors feel
wanted and loved. Sometimes milder Moses David letters were read to the visitors and babes. Once I questioned why I wasn't allowed to hear the letters reserved
for the older brothers and sisters. Steven explained:
"The Bible says not to feed strong meat to babes. Babes
need the milk of the Word." So I patiently bided my
time until I reached the state of spiritual maturity when
I could listen to the "heavy" letters.

The Family's society was stratified, with a strict hierarchy. The carrot of promotion to a higher level was constantly dangled before us. Only the unquestioning and the zealously loyal, however, were rewarded.

Before bed there was a special time set aside for filling out "tribe reports." These were personal reports detailing any problems we were having, and Scriptures and Moses David letters which we were reading and memorizing. There was a strict quota on the reading and memorizing. Memorizing Moses quotes was not in vogue then; that came later, after we had learned to regard the Moses letters as having just as much divine inspiration and authority as the Bible. The section of the report dealing with the personal problems was always of great interest to the older brothers and the shepherd. This was one way to keep their fingers on the pulse of our lives.

I often wondered about Moses David and what authority he had. The answers came very slowly. I had been visiting the Family for several months before Moses' name was even mentioned. Sometimes, after the inspiration sessions, the Family gathered around while Steven read passages from a small notebook. I was told they were "letters of counsel from a friend." These letters, sometimes with sexual overtones, made me feel uncomfortable, but I shrugged them off as inconsequential.

I had no knowledge that this "friend" or his letters had any control over the Family or the individual members of the colonies. I was to learn all that at a time of the Family's choosing. By that time, I believed what they told me.

5
No Thought for Tomorrow

"Wake up! Praise the Lord! Rise and shine! It's a new morning for Jesus!"

With great effort I opened my eyes. They seemed to be glued tightly shut. My body ached with fatigue. It was a major feat to drag myself into an upright position.

The bright early morning sunshine, streaming through the window and reflecting off the yellow painted walls, dazzled my tired eyes. All I wanted to do was to close them and drift back to sleep.

I got up and pulled on the clothes I had worn the day before—the same faded blue denim skirt and top that I had brought with me when I moved in four months ago. They were old and shabby now, but they would have to do. The Family provided no money for new clothes.

I had been sent by my shepherd to Cork, in the south of Ireland, to help the brethren pioneer a colony in that city. Someone had given us the use of a summer cottage nestled among the cliffs. The view was stunning. Beyond the stark stones and jagged rocks lay a brilliant blue body of water which flowed peacefully out to meet the sea. The cottage afforded an expansive view of the sea and the distant horizon.

The summer cottage was pretty, but practical only as a summer residence. It was unsuited for year-round use by a dozen people.

There were only three bedrooms. The shepherds (or leaders), Solomon and Leah, slept in the front bedroom. The only other sister, Ruth, and I slept in the back bedroom, and two of the newer brothers slept in the third. We were the fortunate ones—we had beds. The other brothers had no choice but to sleep on the floor in the tiny living room. The bedrooms, bathroom, and the small kitchenette all opened out into this area.

I prayed, memorized my Bible verses, and dragged myself out to the living room for morning devotions. Solomon was exhorting the flock on a prophetic passage of the Scriptures.

"God has called us through Moses David to warn the world of wickedness, to give them the message—'Repent or perish.' If we don't do the job, God will hold us accountable for their souls and their blood will be on our hands. When God's judgments come down, the Bible says that the sea will turn red with the blood of innocent people condemned to hell because we didn't give them the message that could save them."

Ours was a heavy burden of responsibility and our serious faces reflected it.

For breakfast, Ruth served thin, watery oatmeal with tea and big chunks of cheap white bread bought at the day-old bakery. Today there was margarine for our bread.

This was a new colony, and there was a lack of "interested businessmen" who were willing to donate food and money. The mother colony in Dublin had supplied us with oatmeal and strained baby fruit. Now and then some of the leaders traveled down to visit us, bringing spiritual inspiration and some meat and cheese to supplement our food supply. Between visits we had to be content with a meager menu. Each of us tried to ignore our hunger pangs in an effort to be spiritual, and letters to families at home never hinted at our plight.

Provisioning was the most dreaded assignment in the colony. Unluckily, an older brother named Jesse and I were chosen for the job. We set off on the fourteen-mile walk into town, carrying the memory of our hungry brothers and sisters. If we failed to return with enough food for the day, we were plagued with guilt. So, determined to succeed this time, we put on a bold front and flashed brave smiles as we tried to hitch a ride from the cars that passed infrequently.

Bolstering each other with Bible quotations, we trudged from merchant to merchant. The man who sold bananas had no interest in helping our Christian youth work. But he did give us each a banana which served as our lunch.

The man in the bread factory laughed in our faces and showed us the door. The aroma of the freshly-baked bread was almost more than we could bear. We made our way along the narrow, winding cobblestone streets to the shop of a butcher across town. The butcher was a kindly old man. Last week he had taken one look at our desperate faces and had given us a small package of meat scraps. Perhaps he would help us again. The blazing sun sent rivulets of sweat down my back and I wished I hadn't brought my coat. We crossed over the River Lee and trudged uphill to the butcher shop. The small white sign in the window read "Closed."

Discouraged and guilt-ridden, we perched on the windowsill to catch our breath. Obviously, we weren't "in tune" with God, or we would have known that the shop was closed. So, as on many other days, "we of little faith" turned towards home empty-handed.

On the way back down the hill, we stopped at the bakery outlet and bought a loaf of day-old bread. Jesse didn't have enough money for two loaves, and I hadn't had any money at all since I had joined the Family and "forsaken all my worldly goods."

Our spirits were low as we crossed the bridge. I tried

to be cheerful, as was expected of a good sister.

"Praise the Lord, Jesse! The Lord is my Shepherd and I shall not want . . ."

Was our faith being tried? Our prayers for provisions so often seemed to go unanswered, but we tried to be strong and believe that the "Lord would provide."

The other brethren were out witnessing in the town. Two by two, they approached people on the street and tried to convert them. As Jesse and I came to the main thoroughfare, we spied two of the older brothers. They both looked drained and tired, but brightened when they spotted us.

"Praise the Lord, Jesse and Melita," one of them greeted us with forced enthusiasm. "One soul was saved today."

I tried to appear excited as befitted a spiritually mature sister. It would have been easier if I weren't so tired and hungry.

The two moved on, and Jesse and I sat down to read a few chapters from the Gospels and share the verses we had learned that morning. I had memorized Job 23:12: "I have esteemed the words of his mouth more than my necessary food." Well, that verse was some comfort—at least we had our priorities in order. We prayed together for direction. We felt that God was telling us that our last stop should be Mrs. Quinn, the lady at the vegetable market. She always gave us something.

At the fruit and vegetable market, none of the stall owners seemed interested in helping us. None, that is, except Mrs. Quinn, the plump, middle-aged widow who struggled to support herself and her children by selling vegetables.

She peered at us through thick glasses. "Need more vegetables?" she offered cheerfully. I think she could see we were hungry. "Sorry, but all I can give ye is a few carrots and potatoes. Business 'as been bad today, you see."

"Carrots and potatoes would be fine, Mrs. Quinn," said Jesse quickly, before she could change her mind.

We could make vegetable soup for supper. At least our "faith" had netted a few provisions.

"Mrs. Quinn, do you ever think about Jesus?" queried Jesse. It was his godly duty to minister spiritual things to those who provided for our physical needs.

"Not very often," admitted Mrs. Quinn.

"What do you spend your time thinking about?" probed Jesse gently. He was seeking for some point of contact to demonstrate Mrs. Quinn's need for Christ. He didn't have to wait long.

"Sex."

"What's that?"

"Well, I spend all my time thinking about sex," beamed Mrs. Quinn.

We dropped that subject like a hot potato. Red-faced with embarrassment, we scurried out, clutching our vegetables—back to our haven from the wicked world.

And for months it was the same. No matter how hard we tried, we were never able to bring home enough food. We were shamed for our lack of faith. Out of desperation, we began picking through the big dumpsters behind a large supermarket.

As a well-brought-up young lady in a fairly well-to-do family, I was given no preparation for scavenging food. It took a great deal of biting my lip to work up the courage to open the trash cans—and even more courage to lift out wilted vegetables and stale bread. We bundled this discarded food into old shopping bags or wrapped it in newspapers to take home.

One day I was leaning over the trash bin behind a store when I heard a noise. I looked up and saw the grocer standing in his back door, looking at me reprovingly. I was shocked and shamed, but kept on pulling out carrots and beets.

Although I watched Jesse crumble under the strain and struggled together with him for six months to provide for the Family, we never really became friends. Friendship between members of the Family was difficult because communication was restricted.

We were never allowed to speak to each other of our true feelings. Talking about doubts and problems was tantamount to voicing the thoughts of the Devil, and talking about yourself and your feelings was considered the ultimate selfishness. The Family frowned upon any conversation that didn't center on God, the Mo letters or some other directly related "spiritual" topic. Even our very thoughts were programmed and monitored by the leaders.

In 1973, on his birthday, Moses David made a shrewd move that was to change the course of the Children of God. He received a new revelation which was published for us in a lengthy booklet entitled *The Birthday Warning*.

We gathered around Solomon, our shepherd, eager to hear this latest word from heaven. He read histrionically, shouting now and then for effect, while we cowered in our seats. God was angry at Moses and at us for failing to deliver his message to the world. We would be held responsible for everyone who died in darkness without the word of the Lord sent through Moses David.

Apparently, our efforts to win the world to Christ through personal evangelism were not enough. Moses said that the end was sooner than any of us expected. Because of the shortness of time, we needed a more efficient, mass-oriented approach.

"Distribution of the Mo letters is where it's at!" shouted Solomon, with the enthusiasm of a child who had just stumbled across the secret of the universe. "Let Mo do the preaching and we will be his delivery boys.

That way we can reach more people with the message, and finish our job of warning the world before Jesus comes back. Hallelujah!"

"Hallelujah! Praise the Lord!" we echoed rapturously. We held a prayer meeting and several of the brethren received "messages" from God:

"Yea, this is my servant, David. Hear ye him and obey him," intoned Jesse.

"For he is my chosen and beloved. Obey him and follow him as a light in a dark place lest you, too, suffer the judgments of God," Matthew added solemnly.

And we believed it all.

Gradually, "litnessing" (distributing the Mo letters) largely replaced personal witnessing. The first time we took to the streets with the literature, I broke all expectations, distributing a grand total of ten pamphlets in an hour at ten pence apiece (approximately twenty-five cents). I found it easy to charm people with a bright smile and my Irish brogue. These people seemed willing to donate money to a group they knew nothing about once they heard the phrases "Christian youth group" and "We're helping drug addicts."

In time, the fund-raising became a sophisticated business. Some of us were on the streets from ten to twelve hours a day. Those who excelled were hailed as "shiners" and others were encouraged to emulate them. Those who had low statistics were chided as "shamers." Sometimes a persistent "shamer" was turned out of the colony and told to make it on his own until he could improve his statistics. A shamer was given no money or supplies. "The Lord would supply" all needs if he only had faith. Some zealous shiners were known to distribute seven hundred pieces of literature in one day with a grand total of $175 in one day's time. But it was not unusual to collect fifty to one hundred dollars on a consistent basis. During a four-year period, the Children of God claimed a worldwide distribution of 218,108,922 Mo letters, that represented an income of 4.3 million dollars per month.

The people who had donated their money believed they were contributing to a Christian youth group that helped rehabilitate drug addicts. But there were no free clinics, no professionally staffed counseling centers, and no halfway houses or medical help. What were we doing to help drug addicts? Nothing, except preaching damnation to them if they refused to believe the word of Moses.

The money we collected went directly to our colony shepherd, who kept as little as possible for our living expenses. The largest percentage of the money brought into the colony went to the higher administrative levels, to be spent as they saw fit.

Caught up in the "litnessing fever" that pervaded the Family, I saw distribution as a challenge, and as with any challenge, I was determined to excel. I often spent ten hours a day on the streets and distributed over 300 letters each day, six days a week. I never thought about where the money went after it was sent to the higher administrative levels. I had been taught not to think. Moses had instructed us to regard critical or analytical thinking as the tools of the devil, to be suppressed with mindless repetitions of memorized Bible or Mo verses, or by speaking in tongues.

For several months I traveled with some of the brethren around southern Ireland, living in an old converted bus, preaching and litnessing wherever we went. We washed up in hotel restrooms and scrounged for food. The hardships didn't seem all that hard, and I dismissed the future with a Bible quote, "Take therefore no thought for the morrow" (Matt. 6:34). But I was only sixteen and life was still a game.

6
The
Mo Letters
– – Hotline
to Heaven

Summer came. Solomon received a message from the London headquarters that Ezekiel, a high-ranking leader, would be paying us a visit. The colony bustled and hummed with excitement as we prepared for the arrival of this "anointed vessel of God."

When Ezekiel finally came, I was a little disappointed. I expected a Hollywood type, complete with wild hair, glassy stare, and dramatic oratory. Instead, here was a small, round man with small, round glasses and a cherubic smile. When he spoke, his voice was soft and gentle.

Despite his unimpressive appearance, Ezekiel did have strong magnetism and an undisputed air of authority. He had mingled with the high and the mighty—leaders at the very core of the Jesus Revolution. He sang songs composed by David Berg's own son, Aaron, and roused us into such a spiritual frenzy that our singing could be heard on the other side of the hill. We sat at his feet, eager to catch the crumbs of Mo's latest words. We treasured these pearls, diligently writing them down in our notebooks.

"The Revolution is on the move," he reported. "God is doing new and wonderful things through the Mo letters. Distribution is God's tool for reaching the world and the brethren in England are really getting out the literature. But they need more laborers. I want each of you to seek the Lord's will about joining the work in England."

The vast unknown stretched temptingly before me. I was free to move, to travel, as God led. The idea was intoxicating. When all the others were asleep that night, I crept from my bed and sat by the window, gazing at the stars and straining to hear God's voice telling me what to do. By the pale light of the moon, I leafed through the Family's newsletter, which contained brief messages from colonies scattered all over the world. A report from the colony in Birmingham caught my attention. Many people were visiting the colony and getting saved. Some were even walking in off the streets requesting prayer. Birmingham sounded like a spiritually exciting place. I believed that God was giving me a desire to go there.

When I saw Ezekiel the next morning, I told him that the Lord had placed a desire or "burden" in my heart for Birmingham, England. He nodded approvingly. I interpreted this as a sign of God's approval. Jesse and a new sister named Star also felt the Lord calling them to Birmingham.

So, in the fashion of true pilgrims and strangers on the earth, we packed all of our remaining earthly belongings into backpacks and took to the road.

Rides came slowly for three people with a small mountain of luggage. It took several days to reach Dublin, where we planned to catch the ferry to England. We walked for miles, gratefully accepting rides as often as possible. By night, we were exhausted enough to sleep anywhere.

But a power struggle arose between Jesse and me over the spiritual leadership of our little band. I was, and still am, headstrong and independent, reluctant to follow leadership if I think I can do a better job myself. I was more outgoing and vivacious than Jesse and could receive messages from God at the drop of a hat. Sometimes I saw visions, or scriptures came to mind that I interpreted as the voice of God speaking to me. I felt that I should assume the leadership of the group; Jesse felt otherwise. But because he had been with the family longer and was a few years older than I, he assumed the reins of control. It was he who decided what Mo letters we should read and what God's will was for us. I rebelled against this divine dictatorship, but suffered my frustration in silence as best I could.

At times, when I chafed under his domination, Jesse promptly put me in my place with a Mo quote or a verse of Scripture. I had many things to learn about the role and position of woman in the Family, and Jesse was intent upon teaching me.

We stayed at the Dublin colony for a few days before continuing our journey to Birmingham. Jesse had borrowed a book of Mo letters published for leaders and was proceeding to instruct me on the place of women and leadership within the Family.

We sat on the bare floorboards of an empty storage room. The room was suffused with the late afternoon sun. I watched the lazy particles of dust floating in and out of the shaft of sunlight pouring through the dirty window. Jesse was reading a strongly worded Mo letter entitled *Get It Together.*

The tone of the letter was angry and authoritative. Moses David was rebuking some of the women in the group for withholding sexual services from their husbands. A woman was bound by the law to obey and submit to her husband's wishes whether she felt like it or not. She was an appendage, a helpmeet to her husband and under his authority in everything, particularly in bed. Moses David threatened to force reluctant wives to perform sex before the colony if they refused to comply with their husbands' wishes in private. As Sarah obeyed Abraham, calling him "lord," so should the revolutionary woman obey her husband, honoring him as her lord, or get out of the Family and go back to the Devil—a fate worse than death.

I managed to fake a calm appearance, but I was shaking inside. For the first time since I'd joined the Family, I felt as if my own identity were threatened. Moses was attacking something very near the core of my being: the ability to maintain equality, dignity, and personal freedom within an intimate relationship. I felt that my sensibilities had been violated. My existence as a person with a right to choose and control my life was about to be snatched away. I was not a person, but a thing to be possessed and controlled, and this totalitarian oppression was twisted so as to appear to be the will of God. If I were ever to marry, I would forfeit the last vestige of personal control. I would become a slave. I had heard these doctrines before, but somehow they became horribly real and oppressive in the context of marriage.

I shuddered, preoccupied with my own terror. I could hear Jesse droning on:

"You must die to yourself, Melita. You're too proud," he said. "Too concerned about yourself and what you want. You're going to have to yield to the Lord and let Him break you and mold you into a willing vessel until you have no will or desire of your own but to do His will as revealed to Moses . . ."

"Break, Melita . . ."

"Yield . . ."

"Submit . . ."

"Give yourself up . . ."

Several days later we continued our journey. Jesse had won. I meekly submitted to his leadership, suppressing any natural inclination to think or make decisions on my own. Sometimes I questioned him timidly.

"But why is leadership and obedience so important in the Family?" I asked, remembering the freely structured church groups I had attended.

"Obedience to leadership is one of the basic foundations of this endtime movement of God," he answered. "That's the big difference between the Family and the other so-called Christian groups. Our unity and adherence to leadership is the reason we're getting the job done and they're not. We're an army in a spiritual war. We must all die to ourselves every day and let God control and direct our lives through our leaders for the greater purpose of saving the world."

I must have looked doubtful, for he continued:

"One of the greatest sins in the Bible is what we call Agagism. When Saul was still a young king, the Lord sent Samuel, his spiritual leader, to command him to attack the Amalekites and to destroy them and everything they possessed. Saul did attack and conquer, but he took Agag, the Amalekite king, as a prisoner and kept the best of the sheep, lambs and other animals for himself. When Samuel reproached him, Saul tried to justify himself, claiming he had saved the animals to sacrifice before the Lord. Then Samuel told him that 'to obey is better than sacrifice' (1 Sam. 15:22). Even though Saul had obeyed *most* of what his leader had told him to do, he didn't obey totally and absolutely. Therefore, the Lord took the Kingdom of Israel from him. The same could happen to any of us who don't submit to our leaders."

I couldn't argue with him. I didn't know the Scriptures well enough to realize that the verses and ideas were being taken out of context and misinterpreted. Because he was able to quote from the Bible, I believed him.

I said goodbye to Ireland as we sailed out of Dun Laoghaire harbor. I was leaving my birthplace, my sister, my grandmother, my relations and friends, all my roots, in order to go and preach the gospel to all the world. Moses told us that a true missionary didn't return home. I choked back the tears, since shows of such emotion were not revolutionary. My parents had recently moved to London, and I secretly hoped to get permission to visit them.

Having no money for a cabin, when we grew tired we simply rolled out our sleeping bags beside the drunks in the corridor.

The boat docked in the north of England around 3:00 A.M. A fellow passenger offered us a ride in his car. As we sped along in the dawning light I observed the wild, rugged countryside of Wales as it merged slowly with the neat, orderly fields of England. When we reached Birmingham, we found we had forgotten to bring the address of the local colony. Our patient friend allowed us to continue with him to London. At least we had the London colony's address on the back of the literature.

The Family occupied an old, three-story house in the West End. Rumor had it that they were squatting there. We were greeted at the door with open arms and herded upstairs for some rest. In my zeal, I preferred to get to work distributing the Mo letters to the lost souls roaming the streets of London.

In the literature room I met Manasseh. I remembered him from a visit he had made to the Dublin colony when I was living there. His dazzling smile and confident manner, coupled with his heavy American drawl made him a charismatic figure. As we counted our pieces of literature, he explained the latest Mo letter to me.

"Qadaffi's where it's at now, Sister!" he exclaimed. "The end won't be long in coming."

I had to admit I had no idea who this Qadaffi was.

"Muammar Qadaffi is the president of Libya, in Africa," he explained as we hurried to catch the underground train to Picadilly Circus. "He is a totally devout

Muslim and Mo has had several revelations about him. It seems that he is going to be used mightily by God in these last days. Mo says he may be the 'author of confusion,' the antichrist of Revelation 13, or the 'false prophet' who prepares the way of the antichrist. Qadaffi will either take over the world with the help of Arab oil and the Communists, or he will help the antichrist take over the world and run a satanic world government. Then Jesus will come back.

"Mo says we must make friends with Qadaffi, work with him, and help him. That's God's will for us, just as it was God's will for Daniel and Joseph to work with the system kings of their day. It's the Lord's will that we help the antichrist to power in order to speed up the end of the world and the return of Christ."

I still didn't understand, but I was content to follow submissively, swept along by his galvanic enthusiasm.

I spent over a month at this central London colony. The place buzzed with excitement over the "Qadaffi revelation." Surely it was a sign of the end.

But there were also signs that I was nearing the end of my rope. I was confused. I felt resentful of the all-powerful leaders and disturbed over the teachings about Moses David—who he was, what he claimed to be, and the iron control he held over the Family.

One morning Manasseh took me into the empty room which was used to greet visitors. He produced a booklet of five or six Mo letters. The title on the cover simply read *David*.

"These are the *David* letters," he confided. "They're too strong and heavy for babes, but you're now spiritually mature enough to read them."

And so the mystery unfolded. The *David* letters contained a lot of "direct prophecy." God had revealed to David Berg that he was to be the great and final endtime prophet.

"God has given Moses David the ability to interpret the prophecy concerning the end of the world. Mo says that the antichrist should rise to world power sometime in the 1980's, and the end of the world and Jesus' Second Coming should be around 1993!"

That was hard to swallow. I felt as if I were choking on some of this "strong meat" that had been kept from me as a babe.

"Moses is our shepherd," Manasseh continued. "We were all lost sheep, wandering in a society that has no God except money, and no principles and no love. The church system was failing. Our parents were caught up in the world and society was unjust. Then God raised David up to be our shepherd and guide in accordance with the prophecy of Ezekiel 34."

I read the passage that Moses claimed was a prophecy of himself.

"My sheep wandered . . ." it said, "my flock was scattered upon all the face of the earth, and none did search or seek after them . . . (therefore) I will set up one shepherd over them, and he shall feed them, even my servant David; he shall feed them, and he shall be their shepherd. And I the Lord will be their God, and my servant David a prince among them" (Ezek. 34:6, 23–24).

" 'My servant David,' " explained Mannasseh, "refers to Mo. His legal name is David Berg. But, like Moses of old, he is leading the children of God out of bondage into the promised land. The spirits of Moses and David, along with the spirits of other men of God, enter into Mo's body and speak to him, to help him lead the Revolution. Praise the Lord, Sister! We are God's last effort to save the world."

I smiled, but nagging doubts disturbed me. This was a tall order. Mo was no longer "just a friend who writes us letters" as I had been told in the beginning. He was claiming to be the fulfillment of prophecies that most theologians believe to refer to Jesus Christ. He was claiming absolute spiritual supremacy and authority as the final, latter-day prophet.

But the next statement was even more startling. "The Mo letters are the inspired word of God," Manasseh claimed enthusiastically. "They are actually a continuation of the Bible. They are God's word for today, and must be obeyed. We have our own hot-line to heaven. Listen to what Mo says in this letter called *Old Bottles*:

" 'I want to frankly tell you, if there is a choice between reading your Bible and the Mo letters, I want to tell you that you better read what God is saying today, in preference to what He said 2,000 or 4,000 years ago. Then when you've gotten done reading the latest Mo letters, you can go back to reading the Bible.' "

Mo was claiming too much for himself; it seemed heretical. I needed time to think, away from the constant pounding of Mo's doctrines. I needed time to pray about the truth of his claims and my future with the Family.

I didn't tell anyone I was planning to leave. One night I just took the train to my parents' new home in London instead of returning to the colony.

My parents were in bed when I arrived, but rushed to the door to welcome me.

"Why, it's Chicken-Licken!" cried my dad in amazement.

My mother fussed and clucked over me, asking endless questions and trying to stuff me with soup and crackers, bread and cheese.

It's good to have someplace to come back to to pray and sort myself out, I thought to myself as I snuggled down between the crisp, fresh sheets. My mother always kept my room ready, just in case I ever wanted to come home. The periodic rattle of the passing trains soothed me like a lullaby. I was safe. Here I would have some space and time to collect myself, and to make a decision about Moses David and the Children of God.

Day after day, my mother and father urged me to get out of the house. Sometimes I went shopping with my mother to buy clothes to replace the rags I was wearing. But most of the time I stayed in my bedroom, praying, reading the Mo letters and the Bible. But, above all, I was waiting for some sign from God to reveal the truth about Moses David and give me directions for my life.

"Why have you come home?" inquired my mother gently. "Have you left the Family?"

"No, Mammy, I haven't really left the Family. I needed to get away from them for a while to think and pray."

I didn't tell her about Mo's outlandish claims or his antagonistic attitude toward parents. Nor did I look to my parents for advice or guidance. By this time, I was thoroughly indoctrinated. I believed the Devil might try to influence me through them.

I moped around the house for three or four weeks, never confessing what was bothering me. I grew more and more disheartened and confused. I decided to call the colony, hoping, as I had been taught, that God would speak to me through my leaders.

"God bless you, Sister Melita," Manasseh sounded bright and confident. I envied him for that.

"Manasseh, I'm having problems believing the prophecies about Mo," I said, pleading for some direction.

"Well, Sister, God had to raise up someone, and why shouldn't it be Mo?" he spoke persuasively. "Jesus said we could know prophets 'by their fruits' (Matt. 7:20). All you have to do is look at the fruits of Mo's labor. Thousands of souls have been saved. Our ministry has become a worldwide movement. If the Children of God were not of God, do you think we would be prospering and growing?"

"It's so hard to be really sure," I said in anguish. "Those prophecies are really powerful and heavy. It's hard to believe that Mo is a fulfillment of them."

"You know, Sister," he said firmly, "once God has given you the faith, even for a few moments, to believe that Mo is who he says he is, you will be held accountable. Don't fight against God. Don't go back to the world or the lukewarm Christians, or God will spew you out of his mouth."

We prayed together for God to give me strength and faith, then hung up.

Indecision was slowly tearing me apart. So was the loneliness. Finally, I called Jesse, the person I knew best in the colony. He said he wanted to see me. We made arrangements for him to come to my parents' house the next day.

It was a relief to see his familiar face. He stayed for a few days, sleeping in the spare room. During this time we took long walks in the nearby Epping Forest.

As we strolled along between the ancient trees, Jesse tried to ease my doubts. He showed me the latest Mo letter entitled *Green Paper Pig*.

"Mo is predicting the fall of the dollar, Melita," he said. "Money is an idol for the people in the system. Today, the idol is inflated green paper. And it's becoming so inflated that it's going to explode. You can't stay here in the system, Melita. It will collapse soon and the only chance of survival is to be with God's true Family, led by his true shepherd, Mo. Come back to the colony, Melita, before it's too late."

I followed my shepherd—meekly and submissively—back to the fold.

7
One
Wife
of God

I cocked my head and studied Jesse's face. His expression was decidedly somber.

"To test your loyalty to the movement and your motives for returning to the colony," he began gravely, "the leaders have decided to separate us. It's important that you have come back for the right reasons and not for me."

Jesse was being sent to Birmingham and I was to remain in London. As he left he told me to be a strong soldier for the Lord and King David.

I would miss Jesse and his dedication to the Family that always challenged my own flagging faith. But enough of that! Such thoughts were straight from the Devil! *Our only reason for existence is reaching the world with God's message before it's too late*, I lectured myself sternly. So I threw myself feverishly into the work of litnessing.

The London colony to which I was assigned was headed by a young American couple, Jacob and Mary, who had been among the first members to be trained by Mo himself. Jacob was a man with boundless energy and enthusiasm. Despite his serious attitude toward his leadership role in the Family, his small, round glasses and protruding teeth produced a comical appearance. His wife, Mary, was very young and painfully shy. She kept out of sight most of the time, caring for her two-month-old baby. One day when I was helping her with the baby, she told me about her marriage to Jacob.

"Jacob and I were at a leadership meeting one night. They needed another couple to help pioneer a new colony, so we got married . . ."

The serious implications of her words didn't sink in. I was too busy bouncing the baby on my knees, secretly wishing he were mine.

The crowds milled past, intent on a thousand other duties, ignoring my pleas. Litness was slow today in Ealing Broadway, a suburb of London.

"This is for you," I said brightly, passing a Mo letter to a fair-headed young woman who was pushing a pram.

"What's this for?" she asked, obviously annoyed, her eyes searching the cover for a clue.

"We are a young Christian group who help . . ." I began the usual spiel, but she cut me short.

"Oh, it's Moses David and the Children of God. No, thank you. I'm a Christian. I'll pray for you," she said and quickened her step, disappearing around the corner before I could say another word. I sighed. Another one lost to the Devil.

"It's not going so good then?" a concerned voice inquired. I looked around into the friendly eyes of my litnessing partner. Micah was a man in his early twenties, short, slightly overweight, and with a distinct limp. But he was kind and looked out for me like a big brother.

"It hasn't been a good day for me, either," he shrugged as he looked at the large bundle of unsold Mo letters. "Say, why don't we have a snack? We could read a chapter from the Bible. Maybe that would help."

"Let's do," I agreed, feeling a little guilty about taking

the time from our litnessing duties. But I eased my con-
science by reasoning that since Micah was my older
brother, he would not lead me astray. I felt even guiltier
when we ordered huge pancakes topped with syrup
and whipped cream.

"Thank the Lord for the snack," said Micah, with a
broad grin. He didn't seem to feel guilty at all.

He chose a chapter from the New Testament. We read
the verses aloud. When we finished, neither of us was
in the mood for pushing Mo letters again.

Then Micah suggested we see a movie. Family members don't usually waste their time with worldly
cinemas. But Mother Eve, Mo's wife, had endorsed this
particular one, and that made it legitimate.

We watched in awe as the plot unfolded, revealing
the futuristic city of New York, where the inhabitants
survived by eating recycled human bodies. We believed
it to be a prophetic message of the judgments of God on
a wicked nation. It was going to happen just as Mo
predicted.

When we left the theater, we were so preoccupied by
the profound impact of the movie that we failed to
realize we were late for dinner. When we arrived at the
colony, all the Family members were already in their
rooms, studying Mo letters or writing the daily tribe
reports before bedtime. An ominous silence pervaded
the deserted dining room.

Then the storm hit. Jacob swept into the room in a
rage. He glared at us angrily and loosed a flood of
scathing criticism.

"You know you deserted your posts in the midst of
battle, don't you? God is angry, Brother and Sister. You
failed Him today, and He is rebuking you through me."
His voice rose to a higher pitch. Two of the older
brothers slid into the room to witness the verbal lashing
and psychological humiliation. Later, when they had

their own colonies, they would know how it was done.

Jacob shook his head and began to recite our shortcomings. I was willful. Micah was lazy. I was a flirt. Micah was out of the Spirit.

"You not only wasted God's precious time," he continued, "you wasted His money. Why, that's like stealing from God! You have sinned. You are insensitive to God's voice. You are poor messengers for the Lord and King David."

He turned on me. "As for you, Sister, you should have the humility to lie low after what you have done. You do know what I mean, don't you?" I had an uneasy feeling he wasn't talking about the current misdemeanor.

"You mean because I went home to visit my parents?" I asked meekly.

"That's exactly what I mean. You're a weak sister, Melita. Only weak people leave the Family."

Smarting under his blows, we felt debased and properly chastened. But of course we deserved the reprimand. God was speaking to us through our leader, Jacob. We thanked him and slunk to our respective rooms like children being sent to bed without any supper.

I glanced back at Jacob before I turned the corner. He was smiling proudly and rubbing his hands together. He had succeeded in breaking us a little more, preparing us for the mold of Moses David's perfect will.

The next morning I apologized and promised to be a more obedient and submissive disciple. I had done wrong. I had wasted God's time and money. I was a disgrace to King David. But I would change. I would work harder than ever to get the word to the lost.

"Curse the Church system," Jacob exclaimed one night after reading a Mo letter.

"Why?" I dared to ask, genuinely puzzled. I'd always thought that the Church people were saved even if they weren't as zealous as we.

"*Why?*" he raved in an incredulous tone. "*Why*, you ask me? The so-called 'churches' have failed. They look for the easy life, not the life of sacrifice. They willfully disobey the Bible, which commands us to forsake all and take up our cross daily. We live communally like the early Christians. When we die, Mo says, we will be first-class citizens in the heavenly city. Those lukewarm Christians and Children of God who return to the System will be only pitiful second-class citizens." He paused for breath. His round face was flushed with emotion.

I'd never thought of Christians outside the Family as the opposition. How logical it all seemed now. All believers have one Father, God, and Savior, Jesus Christ. But *we* were the obedient children who would receive the greatest reward. I swelled with a feeling of importance. We, the Children of God, were the elite. Through us and because of our obedience, God's promises and purposes would be fulfilled. Moses David *must* surely be the true endtime prophet.

Though I still had some questions and doubts, I put them quickly out of my mind, confident that God would reveal to me the full truth. In the meantime, I drifted along with the ever-shifting tide.

There was a growing unrest among the colonies scattered about London. The colonies were overcrowded, with as many as thirty or forty people living in one house. This unwieldy number made for sluggish movement. Care of this large group, made it difficult to litness for more than a few hours a day.

Philip, a tall, gangly ex-drama student with great bulbous eyes, was ready to lead an insurrection.

"Look here, all of you," he said one evening after supper, "God has allowed us all to live for the past twenty-four hours. At the most, we have been litnessing for four or five of those twenty-four hours. What did we do with the other twenty hours? Where is our fruit for the Lord? If it is true that our only purpose here on earth is to get God's message through Moses out to the waiting world, why aren't we doing it?"

He looked accusingly from face to face. "Why aren't we spending more of our time on the streets reaching the lost?" He banged the table vehemently. "Why? I'll tell you why. It's because the colonies are too big. They are a curse. We spend all our time eating and taking care of ourselves while lost souls perish on the streets. I'm leaving. I'm going to free myself to get the message out. Anyone who truly wants to serve God and Moses David can come with me."

Philip rushed out of the room and slammed the door, leaving us in stunned, uneasy silence. Maybe he was right. Maybe we were spending too much time on ourselves and not enough on the streets. We felt guilty. Certainly no one wanted to fall out of favor with God or Moses David.

A few days later Philip returned triumphantly. He and several other brothers had been led by God to a coffee shop near Soho, the district of sex-shops and X-rated cinemas. Once again he invited any of us who wanted to obey God completely to come with him. Fired by his enthusiastic challenge, I went.

The coffeehouse was an underground, cellar-like structure situated at the end of an alley. One side of the alley was a brick wall. On the other side, above our cave, was a gay bar. A rusty sign with a Siamese cat and the words "Members Only" was the only outside indication that the establishment existed.

We christened our coffeehouse "Heidi's Cave" after a recent Mo letter. Whatever we lacked in material resources we made up in vigor and enthusiasm. We lived out of our backpacks, slept on the floor, and spent from early morning until late at night litnessing on the streets or witnessing to people who came by the coffeehouse.

We read the Mo letters daily for our inspiration and gradually lost touch with the London leadership.

Often, we litnessed late into the night, firmly believing that "God . . . commanded the light to shine out of darkness . . . to give the light of the knowledge of the glory of God . . ." (2 Cor. 4:6). The shrivelled, shrunken, green-pallored junkies became a common sight. It didn't do much good to give them Mo letters or try to talk to them, for many times they were too far gone to understand what was being said to them. Night after night I watched the police load them, screaming, into shiny black vans and take them away. I felt helpless and wanted to believe there was some answer to all this misery. Moses David said he had the answers. I believed him and plugged the letters with even more zeal.

A message was issued from the central headquarters which halted us in our tracks. Everyone was to meet at the West End colony that afternoon.

We returned to the colony expecting to be punished for our insurrection. We sat demurely, waiting for the meeting to begin, praying that God would have mercy on our rebellious souls.

Two of the top female leaders were in charge of the meeting—Esther, the wife of Mo's son, Hosea—and Joy, who I learned was one of Mo's wives. A hush fell over the room as they entered and the lesser disciples respectfully made way for them. The hour had come. God was about to speak through His handmaidens.

Joy strummed her guitar delicately, setting the mood for her plaintive song. "We must work together to save the lost for whom Jesus wept," she sang.

During the silence that followed, she produced a new Mo letter and held it up for us to see.

The title stood out in bold type! *One Wife*. Beneath the caption I could make out a sketch of a man sitting in a large, old-fashioned bed, surrounded by several pretty young women.

"This is the voice of God speaking to us," said Joy emphatically. "We have been going our separate ways, especially you with the coffeehouse. God stresses in this letter that He wants us to be a unified Family, His bride."

The message of the letter was simple and straightforward. We were to be melded together in one unit instead of many. Collectively we were to be the "one wife" of God.

We were stricken with guilt. As a sign of our repentance we closed the coffeehouse and returned to the colony, ready once again to follow our leaders.

8
The Christmas Monster

Soon I was transferred to the Liverpool colony where, once again, I was thrust among strangers whom I was obliged to embrace as brothers and sisters. The English cities were larger and with more anonymity than the small Irish towns of my childhood. More and more, I was losing touch with my past and the old country and often felt lost and lonely in the midst of the Family.

The constant movement of people among the colonies made close, long-term relationships difficult. It wasn't unusual to go to sleep beside a sister, only to awaken and find her gone. It was unrevolutionary to ask "Why?" "The only things you can be sure of," we were told, "are the Lord, hard work, constant change—and joy!"

Ah, joy. That elusive absolute that I had been promised but had never found . . .

However, in Liverpool, I was at least given a chance for some personal fulfillment. Because of my father's experience in printing, it was assumed that I might have some natural skills. So I was made deaconess over the printing of the Mo letters.

The printing machinery was housed in our garage. I was taught to make plates, to run the machinery, and to oversee the entire operation. The print shop was my domain. Here I was free to be my own boss, free to be creative and productive. Many times I worked late into the night to prepare a rush order of Mo letters. But I didn't mind. I loved the constant rumble of the machines and thrived on the satisfaction of competently performing skilled work.

One Thursday afternoon I was concentrating on making some plates when Zion, our colony shepherd, came striding in.

"How's it going, Melita?" he asked, brushing his heavy mop of blonde hair out of his eyes.

"Fine, Zion," I said, without looking up from the plates.

"You know, Melita, you're doing good work here. You're on fire. I'm glad you're in our colony."

Gratefully, I flashed him a smile. I liked Zion. He made me feel good about myself. I stopped to hear what he had to say.

"Melita, I've some good news for you. Some important messages need to be delivered to the Birmingham colony right away. You and Habakkuk are to hitchhike down there tomorrow and deliver them."

Early Friday morning, Hab and I set off for Birmingham. We sat by the side of the road, singing revolutionary songs while we waited for a ride. It was a warm, sunny day and we hadn't been waiting long when a pleasant young man in a two-door sedan stopped to pick us up.

I climbed in the back seat, thanking him profusely, while Hab slid into the front seat. I noticed the seat belt dangling out the door and thoughtlessly reached for it. Unfortunately, Hab picked that precise moment to slam the door shut. I yelped in pain.

"What's the matter, Melita?" he asked, tugging harder on the door handle before turning around to see what I wanted.

"My finger, my finger!" I screamed. "You've shut the door on my finger! Open the door!"

When my dilemma finally registered with him, Hab flung the door open and I retrieved my battered and bloody hand. There was an ugly laceration. The skin was torn from the underside of my middle finger, leaving exposed some white bone and membrane. I was too stunned to feel pain.

"Dear God," prayed Hab, the blood draining from his face.

Our ill-fated friend took command of the situation and sped us to the hospital where I was rushed into surgery. When I came to in a stark, sterile room, Hab was hovering over me.

"Melita, Melita," he crooned. "What a beautiful sister you are."

I promptly burst into tears, not because I was in pain, but because I had failed again. One of the teachings that Mo had drilled into his flock had to do with miraculous healing. If one had faith, doctors and hospitals were unnecessary. Obviously, I didn't have enough faith. Once again I had failed God, the Family, and Moses David.

There were new and ominous moves within the leadership structure. Mo now decreed that the different operations of the colonies should be delegated to councils of leaders. So, my beloved job as literature deaconess was abruptly snatched away. I was told to pray for another post. The great unknown that had appeared so inviting in the days of cozy Cork now loomed lonely and frightening.

As I evaluated my new status, I realized how awkward and out of place I felt. Though I was only sixteen, by colony standards I was now considered an older sister—and an *unmarried* older sister at that! There didn't appear to be any place for a single sister like myself. At that moment my loneliness and feeling of uselessness far outweighed my former fierce pride and independence. The idea of a husband was more appealing than it had ever been. I needed someone to care for me and give me a reason for being. I would bide my time until God sent a man. Then I could take my place beside the married sisters of the Revolution.

Teams from the other colonies in Northern England were constant visitors. They came to pick up literature from our presses.

I was reassigned to the kitchen now, a job which gave me an opportunity to talk to many who passed through for a snack and some conversation. I always asked questions about the locations of the various colonies and what they were accomplishing there for the Lord. Surely God would give me a clue as to my own future.

One evening a familiar figure burst into the kitchen. It was Seth, a brother from the Dublin colony.

"Seth! I didn't know you were in England!"

"It's good to see you, Melita," he said, kissing my cheek and giving me a crushing bear hug. "Peter and I are pioneering a colony in Sheffield. God is getting out the lit there. The place is bursting at the seams with lost sheep, ripe and ready for the words of Moses David."

"Sounds like a great place to be," I said longingly.

"You know, we two klutzy brothers could use a pretty sister to do the cooking for us and brighten up the place," he invited.

I accepted on the spot, rationalizing that this must be God's will. My leaders agreed. What else could they do with me?

Sheffield, the city of steel, was a sprawling, smelly place, but it was good litnessing territory. It was easy to sell over 300 pieces of literature in a day. Kind people gave us places to stay at night. We often provisioned our meals in restaurants, or bought fish and chips and munched them as we walked.

After several weeks of living on the road, we decided that we were spending too much time looking for places to sleep. If we had a place of our own, we reasoned, we could concentrate on litnessing.

Five minutes from the heart of the city, we found several rooms for rent in a boarding house. I took the smaller room on the second floor beside the bathroom, and the boys moved into the finished attic. We shared the bathroom and kitchen with the other tenants. The mattresses were old and worn, the bedclothes tattered, the paint cracked in many places, and the wallpaper was faded. But it was home for us. From this base we could spread out and win Sheffield for Jesus and Moses David.

We quickly set up a schedule that would allow us maximum time on the streets for litnessing. We rose at six in the morning and rushed out to "hit the schools." Every morning we took a bus to a different school and hung around until the kids began to arrive. Then we saturated them, from the youngest to the oldest, with the Mo letters. Mo instructed us to aim specifically for the younger kids who were more impressionable and willing to believe than their elders. When asked to donate money to our cause, many of them gave us their lunch money.

Jubilantly tallying our money for the morning, we hurried home for breakfast and study to strengthen ourselves for the rest of the day's activities. We devoured the Mo letters. These words were spiritual nourishment. We would be sure to need it before the day was out.

Litnessing in Sheffield was often a battle of wits against the English "bobbies" or police. We had no license to collect money on the streets. Consequently, it was in our own best interest to avoid the police. If we were caught, as some of us were from time to time, we were charged with illegal selling on the streets, brought to court, and fined. Avoiding the police didn't pose an insurmountable problem. In England, the tall, rounded helmets worn by the policemen made them easy to spot above a crowd. We were careful to keep a wary eye out, and when we saw them, warn our litnessing partner and run. According to Mo, we were doing nothing illegal or immoral. After all, God was on our side. We were simply obeying "the laws of God rather than the laws of man."

Seth was our shepherd, our leader, our spiritual authority. Peter and I were his sheep and were expected to follow him mindlessly.

An impetuous American, Seth was sadly lacking in patience and common sense. He generally rushed from activity to activity, often without thinking and many times with disastrous results. At times he was oppressively domineering.

One day, on our way to go litnessing, we were passing through the living area when he noticed some rubbish on the sideboard.

"Melita, that rubbish shouldn't be there. Pick it up and put it in the trash." He was testing me.

I balked. How dare he speak to me like that!

"You really don't like to be under authority, do you?" he said sternly, then sighed in frustration.

I lowered my eyes submissively, secretly staring with contempt at his skinny legs and the hole in the knee of his blue jeans.

I picked up the rubbish, carried it into the kitchen and threw it violently into the trash can. I felt as if I were throwing away my self-respect with the garbage.

In September, 1973, panic struck. "The Christmas Monster," as Moses had dubbed the great comet, Kohoutek, was on its way. It was an omen of doom, heralding the long-awaited collapse of America and the end of the world. Mo predicted that something terrible would happen around January 31st, strongly suggesting that date as America's doomsday.

We had only a few months to warn the wicked. Huge quantities of the "Kohoutek" letter were printed and mass-distributed with single-minded fanaticism. As January 31st approached, our sense of urgency increased. We litnessed feverishly, and began to prepare for the impending catastrophe that would surely come if the final end of things didn't.

Our leaders gave us precise instructions for "survival storage." We stockpiled food, water, and other necessities in the colonies so we could survive the expected chaos. We provisioned all the non-perishable goods we could, and bought canned goods at a discount warehouse. In the attic we stored burlap bags of grain and beans. Outside the house we filled huge drums with water.

I wrote to warn my aging grandmother that the end was near. America's days were numbered, and if she were going to survive, she'd better stock up on canned food.

Nobody planned beyond the 31st of January—D-Day. We interpreted everything in the news as another sign of the end and confirmation of the Mo letters.

Then it happened.

The comet fizzled out. No chaos, no confusion. Business in America went on as usual.

Of course, we did not voice our questions, but Mo had a lot of explaining to do. He opted for a viable alternative to admitting he was wrong; he blamed us. We were the ones who had misinterpreted what God had said. Mo had never said America was going to fall on the 31st of January; he had merely suggested it was possible. "I'm only a man," he said, "and as a man my suggestions can be wrong." But we knew better. It was the unwritten law that the true disciples believed Mo implicitly in everything, including his "suggestions." To challenge his decrees could result in excommunication from the true Family of God. Consequently, we chose to believe him—and gladly accepted the blame when he was wrong.

9
Slave-Wife

Festive Christmas lights twinkled in shop windows. Lamp posts wore garlands of greenery and bright holly berries. The scene was straight out of Charles Dickens' Christmas classic.

Everywhere I looked, young couples strolled arm in arm, some laden with gaily-wrapped treasures, others laughing merrily with secrets of the season. It seemed this year that all the shoppers came in pairs! How I envied the happy couples who had someone to share this special time. My loneliness became a physical ache.

In my unhappy state, my thoughts turned more and more often to Seth. Despite his sometimes oppressive leadership and thoughtlessness, he was a handsome man. His crystal-clear blue eyes often pierced mine and held them captive. There was a hint of mischief in his broad smile, and his playful antics kept my spirits high.

One night, as I was typing our weekly report to the leaders, Seth came into the kitchen to keep me company. I noticed that he was nervous and jittery, sitting on the edge of his chair and drumming his fingers on the table. It was late and I wanted to get the report done so I could get to bed. The kitchen was small and confining and his nervousness began to annoy me.

"Seth," I begged, "why don't you go to bed and leave me to finish this report in peace?"

"I don't feel like turning in just yet," he hedged.

"Really, I could finish up much quicker by myself."

"Uh, Melita," he cleared his throat. "I've something to tell you. I mean . . . the Lord has shown me something . . . you need to know."

"Well, what is it?" I snapped, picking up my typing speed.

"I was praying the other day and the Lord told me . . ." He broke off the sentence, either searching for the right words or the courage to say them.

"Well?" I was losing my patience at this point. "What did the Lord tell you?"

"I was praying for a wife. I really need a wife, you know. And the Lord just said, 'Why don't you marry Melita?' " He grinned shyly and waited for my answer.

My fingers stopped dead on the keys. I stared at him blankly. Although I was lonely, I was terrified by the thought of losing—in marriage—any more of my personhood.

"The Lord hasn't shown me anything about that, Seth," I finally said. "At least—not yet."

In the days that followed, he was unusually kind and attentive. It was becoming more and more difficult to resist his awkward attempts at courtship. But I succeeded—for awhile.

The day started out badly. I awoke feeling queasy and, as the day wore on, I developed acute abdominal cramps that left me doubled up in pain. Taking an aspirin was out of the question, since resorting to medication of any kind indicated a lack of faith.

Seth and I left the house to do some litnessing, while Peter made the trip to Liverpool for more literature. But I litnessed very poorly.

In the middle of the afternoon, Seth suggested we stop for a snack so that I could rest. I was tired and discouraged. He put his arm around me and led me gently into a sidewalk café. After pork pies and tea, we sat and talked. Seth seemed genuinely concerned about my illness.

The pain lowered my defenses. I needed someone who cared. I needed some strength. And Seth was there, more than willing to provide everything I needed.

At that moment, he seemed so different from the rude, overbearing leader of our little group. Warm feelings bubbled inside. I saw only his reassuring smile and felt his concern for my well-being. I heard him saying he loved me. All the things I had so deeply resented about him seemed unimportant.

So this was what it was like to fall in love!

I floated out of the café, clutching Seth's arm. Outside, the street lights twinkled magically, casting bright reflections on the wet city streets. I skipped along, my pain forgotten, distributing Mo letters to weary shoppers, shivering in their overcoats. I didn't feel the cold at all.

During the next few weeks, Seth and I rode the crest of an emotional high. We rushed to be together each morning, and begrudged the time that litnessing kept us apart. I was blinded to his faults. It was enough that we were together and that he cared for me.

Three weeks after Seth had first proposed, I moved upstairs to his bedroom. It never occurred to either of us that we were doing anything immoral. Mo teaches that there is no such thing as "premarital sex," since sex is synonymous with marriage in God's eyes. I failed to see the irony of this teaching, and wrote in my Bible that we were married on December 8, 1973, by God Himself, with a host of heavenly helpers as our witnesses.

We didn't tell the leadership that we were living together. I was so afraid of losing the magic. If they knew, our relationship would be subject to the rules of the Family, and I would be forced to submit to the status of a servant, obeying Seth's every command, with the leaders watching constantly to make sure I did. For a few weeks, we were able to keep our romance a secret. But our days of bliss were numbered.

The day before my seventeenth birthday, all the colonies were summoned to a hotel in Manchester to observe a real Family-style Christmas celebration. Christ's birth would not be demeaned by the idolatrous worship of Santa Claus.

As the pilgrims continued to pour in from the scattered colonies, the women busied themselves preparing a huge Christmas dinner from boxes of food donated by generous merchants. As we worked, we repeated Bible verses and Mo quotes, sometimes gasping at their spiritual significance.

By suppertime, everyone had arrived. The festive spirit grew as Joy, our leader, led in rousing songs and dances. Brothers grabbed sisters and swung them around in time to the music. Seth dragged me from the kitchen to join him in the dancing.

After our sumptuous feast, we gathered in a cozy, candlelit room to hear a Mo letter entitled *Spirit Tree*. Joy had promised that it would reveal the true spirit of Christmas. In the letter, Mo ridiculed conventional Christmas traditions and those who practiced them. "All I want for Christmas," he wrote, "is Jesus."

Our bodies, unaccustomed to rich food, were soon sated with the large meal we had consumed. Now, in the drowsy state that follows overindulgence, we glowed with the impact of Mo's words. We were, indeed, God's elite, safely removed from the misconceptions of the pagan world.

We joined hands as Joy led in prayer. "Lord, we thank you for our King David and that through him we can know the true meaning of Christmas. Lord, thank you for the bountiful meal You provided for us tonight, and for all the precious sisters who prepared it. Thank you for giving us women to be helpmeets for the men . . ."

Seth giggled.

Joy opened her eyes.

"Seth, why are you laughing?"

He didn't reply, but cast a nervous glance in my direction.

She smiled knowingly. All the leaders were aware of our attraction for each other. She closed her eyes and finished her prayer, then waited silently for the Lord to speak.

Several people quoted Bible verses that defined proper man-woman relationships.

Joy opened her eyes. They were glittering with excitement.

"The Lord has revealed that Seth and Melita should be married," she announced.

All eyes were upon us.

"Seth, do you really want to take Melita as your wife?" Joy asked.

"Yes . . . I do," Seth stuttered.

"Melita, do you want to have Seth as your husband?"

The newborn baby in her arms woke up. As she rocked the child back to sleep, she looked at me again and asked, "Are you ready for this?" She pointed to the baby.

I nodded dumbly, not realizing I was already pregnant.

"The Lord is very generous with babies in the Revolution. We need more children to grow up to be soldiers for Jesus and David. If you both agree, then we will pray over you and you will be wed in the sight of God."

Everyone gathered around and laid their hands on us. Joy read some Scriptures as I stood there dazed, not believing what was happening and incapable of stopping it.

"Wives, submit yourselves unto your own husbands, as unto the Lord . . . Husbands, love your wives . . ." (Eph. 5:22, 25).

I choked back the tears. My greatest fear had come to

pass. I was being signed away, given into slavery. From now on I would belong to my husband. He controlled me, his leaders controlled him, and Moses controlled all of us.

"A ring, a ring!" cried Joy. "Does anyone have a ring for the newlyweds?"

Someone handed her a man's ring. It was a broad gold band with a square top and a diamond in one corner. No one had a woman's ring to offer. Joy slipped the ring on Seth's finger.

The deed was done. We were man and wife in the eyes of the Family.

The next morning there were snickers, knowing glances, and nudges as we came downstairs. I cornered Joy with a battery of questions.

"Joy, how does the Family feel about legal marriages? Should Seth and I get a marriage license? What should I tell my parents?"

She smiled at me condescendingly.

"A legal marriage license is only a piece of paper. But if you want to get one, it's up to you. As for telling your parents, that depends on your own faith."

I telephoned my parents collect. They wanted me to come home for Christmas. I asked if I could bring one of the brethren along with me. That was fine, too. I told my mother I was bringing Seth, that nice young American she had met in the Dublin colony.

We traveled by bus and train to my parents' house the very same day. We ate my mother's cooking until we could eat no more. For the rest of the evening, we sat in the living room watching TV, chatting, and sipping my father's homemade port.

"Well, it looks like it's time to turn in," said my father, yawning and winding his watch.

My mother began to put away her knitting.

Seth and I stole furtive glances at each other. Who

was going to break the news? And what should we say?

Silently, I prayed for strength. *Lord, help them accept Your will.* It *was* God's will, of course. The leaders had confirmed it through their visions.

"Uh, Mr. McManus," Seth cleared his throat, "if you could wait a bit, we have something to tell you."

"Yes, what is it?" He sat down again.

"Well . . ." he paused. "You see, uh, your daughter and I are married."

My mother was shocked. My father struggled to maintain his composure.

I refused to look at either of them and deafened myself to my mother's sobs. I fished around in my bag and produced my wedding ring. It was a cheap gold band, hastily purchased in a second-hand store. Defiantly, I slipped it on the third finger of my left hand.

"Well, Chick," said my Dad, "I trust you've given the matter considerable thought and know what you are doing."

"Oh, yes, Daddy," I lied. "We're very sure that our marriage is God's will."

My mother was not easily consoled. "Do you have a license?" she asked. "You're not . . . well . . . sleeping together without being legally married, are you?"

"We don't need a stupid piece of paper," we chimed. "Our marriage is sealed in heaven."

Nevertheless, Seth was asked to sleep in the guest room until we could "legalize" our relationship.

We came. We saw. We crushed their expectations and caused them pain, then returned to our *real* Family. After all, we were doing the Lord's will. But we were legally married in Sheffield on the 11th of January, 1974, and I took my place beside Seth as the shepherd's wife, helping him run the little colony which had grown to seven disciples.

10
The
Outlaws

Morning dawned, and with it, a strange, uneasy sensation in the pit of my stomach. The thought of food was revolting. Waves of nausea ebbed and flowed until I had to make an abrupt exit from the morning Mo studies. When this procedure became a daily occurrence, I realized that I was most definitely pregnant!

At first, Seth was overjoyed with the news. I had no choice in the matter since birth control was not allowed, but secretly I was pleased. Besides, women were created to bear children, we were taught.

"We need more children to strengthen the Revolution," Mo had written. "Children are the promise of the future."

As I grew weaker from the relentless attacks of nausea and vomiting, Seth's attitude toward me changed.

"What's the matter with you, Melita? Don't you have any faith at all?" he shouted one day after I had thrown up for the third time. "If you would only pray, God would heal you. The leaders are beginning to complain about your low litnessing statistics. You can't go on like this."

He was right. I couldn't. No matter how hard I prayed, the morning sickness which stretched into the evening hours, was worse, if anything. Exhausted most of the time, I clutched at any excuse to skip litnessing and sleep.

In frustration, Seth telephoned Joy to report my strange behavior and to ask what he should do.

"Joy said you must eat," he called, bursting into the bedroom where I was trying to rest. "She says if you eat enough at the right times, you won't feel so nauseous."

Seth dragged me out of bed and down to the street to a cheap café. He ordered two grilled lamb chops, boiled carrots, and mashed potatoes and ordered me to eat.

I tried to be obedient, but the smell of the food turned my stomach. I sat there, gagging on cold lamb chops, with tears streaming down my face. Seth was adamant. "You're going to sit there until you've eaten everything on that plate," he insisted. "That's what the leaders said to do and that's what you're going to do."

People in the café stared. The kindly proprietress glanced at me with concern but didn't dare interfere.

When I had forced down the food to his satisfaction, Seth decided that we should go litnessing. It was already dark and I was tired. I begged to go home to bed.

"Don't you care about the lost souls dying without the words of life from Moses David?" he chided. "Are you so self-centered these days that you can think of nothing but your own needs? The Lord will give you the strength if you obey."

I followed him meekly into town. Half-heartedly, I passed out a few Mo letters, and when he wasn't looking, I slipped into the ladies' room and threw up.

During those first few months of pregnancy, I felt utterly discouraged and depressed and often crawled off by myself to cry. Sometimes Seth found me and berated me for being so weak and unspiritual.

The situation was growing serious. Seth was powerless to control his wife. Leaders were called in to "counsel" me and find out what sin was at the root of my problem.

"Melita, if you don't have the faith to overcome this sickness," one leader warned severely, "you're not going to make it in the Revolution. Your weak faith is resulting in physical weakness. There are many other pregnant sisters in the Family who have not let their condition interfere with their service for the Lord. They have the faith to stay well."

Despite this warning, I continued to feel weepy, nauseous, and tired until the third month when suddenly, as so many other mothers know, my body became accustomed to the change. I began to feel like a human being again.

But it was too late. During my months of spiritual malaise, my "lack of faith" had affected the entire colony. The statistics were at a pitiful low and all seven of our disciples had backslidden and left the Family. We had failed miserably as colony leaders.

More trouble arrived in the form of two of the top London leaders—Joy, and a sassy young American she was training by the name of Zebedee. They made it clear that they had come to straighten us out.

We were ordered to the living area for a disciplinary session. Since Seth was the leader, Zebedee started in on him first.

"I'm beginning to wonder if you really have a shepherd's heart at all, Seth." He began to speak in a normal tone which soon escalated in tone and tempo. "This colony is dead. All your sheep were so sick of you that they left. You'd better become a responsible soldier. After all," he pointed at me as I sat sniveling on the couch, awaiting my turn, "you are going to be a father in a few months."

Seth's face registered defeat. Zebedee's scathing indictment had reduced him to a mindless nodding yesman.

"And you, Melita, how do you account for the disaster this colony has become?"

I gathered all my courage and spoke up.

"I don't believe the Lord wanted a colony in Sheffield. I believe He wanted us to move on to a new city, so he didn't bless us here."

"Listen here, Sister," he roared, his dark eyes flashing with anger. "That's an excuse for your own sin and departure from God. That is murmuring against the Lord. Sister, you'd better get right with God or you're going to be sorry."

We were sent to our room to pray and repent of our sins. I felt I had played this scene before.

In much the same way as after the rebuke by Jacob in London, I crawled to Zebedee the next morning, confessing my guilt, begging forgiveness and promising to do better.

Zebedee grabbed me by the waist and crushed me against him. My body was rigid.

"Loosen up! Loosen up!" he commanded. "That's more like it. That's how a real revolutionary sister gives her brother a hug."

"Hey, Seth," he called, "how is she in bed?"

"Oh . . . fine!" laughed Seth, with embarrassment.

"Maybe you need to improve, Sweetie," he said. "Unless you loosen up and stop being such a prude, you'll never be able to take the changes that are coming."

I had no idea what he was talking about.

Our colony was handed over to another couple. Seth and I were openly disgraced in the Family news bulletin and turned out of the colony to live by faith on the road. We were given no money or supplies. "We won't be able to hitchhike and live on the streets," I protested. "I'm pregnant."

If we had the faith, we were told, the Lord would provide.

We spent several months traveling from city to city,

scrounging for food and a place to sleep at night.

In the historical town of King's Lynn in East England, we met a Christian woman who owned a hotel. We could be very agreeable with Christians when it suited us. It was to our advantage to cultivate her good will. So we sat for hours and talked to her, convincing her of the fine work we were doing with young people. She often gave us meals and let us stay at her hotel free of charge.

We spent our days litnessing on the streets of King's Lynn, and soon became familiar fixtures on Main Street, hustling people as they passed by. Whenever either of us saw a policeman, he warned the other, hastily hid the Mo letters, and walked casually down the street pretending to be window shopping.

One day Seth wasn't quick enough. A policeman, tipped off by his wife, caught Seth red-handed.

"Hey there, laddie, what 'ave you got there?"

"Oh, just some Christian literature," grinned Seth, innocently. I felt uncomfortable as a curious crowd began to gather.

"Well, laddie, you're American, are yeh?"

"Yes, sir. I am, sir," replied Seth courteously, hoping to appease him.

The policeman took one of the Mo letters and leafed through the pages.

"Do you sell this Christian literature, then?" he asked still browsing through the literature.

"No, sir. Not at all, sir," Seth lied.

"What's this, then, on the cover that says 'Suggested Donation—Ten Pence'?" probed the policeman.

"Well, that doesn't mean we sell the literature," Seth manipulated his words very carefully. "But we do ask for donations."

"What kind of license do you have for this work?"

"We have a license from God," Seth beamed. "Our work saves young people from lives of sin and uselessness."

"That's all fine and good," the policeman was getting impatient now, "but where's your license to collect money? Do you have one?"

"No," Seth admitted.

"Well then, laddie, you'd better come down with me to the station. And if this is your wife, she'll 'ave to come along, too."

We walked silently behind our captor, as the onlookers whispered among themselves. Someone laughed. I felt humiliated and was near tears. But Mo had taught us that concern for our reputation was sinful pride. We should be willing to suffer social rejection and ridicule if necessary.

We were led into a small, miserable room for questioning. There was a Gideon Bible on the windowsill, and a few battered metal chairs. The policeman who had brought us in stood behind a wooden desk and asked for our passports. He checked the expiration date on my passport and handed it back to me. Irish passport holders can come and go without a visa in England. But when he leafed through Seth's American passport, his brow furrowed in a dark frown.

"What's this, then? Your English visa expired months ago. Do you realize you are in this country illegally?" His tone was very serious now.

"I . . . I guess I forgot to get it renewed," Seth offered lamely.

"Well, laddie, I'm booking you on two charges. One: hawking on the streets without a proper license, and two: violation of visa requirements."

We gasped in horror. The Lord couldn't be allowing this to happen to us. After all, we were only following orders.

We walked out of the police station clutching the notice of Seth's court date, dazed with disbelief, and overcome with shame and guilt. Not only had we failed as colony shepherds, but now we had brought disgrace and the law down on the Family. With trembling fingers we dialed our leadership for direction.

Our blunder caused a furor. This kind of exposure could only hurt the work of God and Moses David. Seth and I cowered under the scathing rebuke. Only people who were out of touch with God got caught litnessing. This was the judgment of God which He had sent because we were out of tune with Him. We had better repent quickly and immerse ourselves in the Mo letters. We were spiritually weak. Failures.

Two smooth-talking leaders came up from London to advise us about the court case. Matthew, former insurance executive, had been among the first twelve disciples in Europe. He had left his job to serve the Lord full time. His partner, Philip, was a younger man—shrewd and glib. He had been a con artist and thief. Together, they drilled Seth to prepare him for his court appearance.

When the day came, Matthew and Philip escorted Seth into the courtroom. They were dressed in sedate business suits and had loaned Seth some respectable clothing. Matthew spoke confidently and authoritatively to the Judge:

"Your honor, we are a group of devout Christians. We spend our time helping young drug addicts, alcoholics, the destitute, the vagrant and the unloved. We give our lives bringing the love and salvation of Christ to these people. We distribute our literature free, but do sometimes accept donations. I apologize for the over-zealousness of this young disciple in soliciting donations and harrassing people. I assure you, he will be counseled to temper his zeal."

It worked. Seth got off with a six-pound fine for hawking without a license. The matter of his expired visa was not treated so lightly. He was given several days to leave the country.

We returned to London with Matthew and Philip,

where we waited for the leaders to decide our fate. We were the naughty children who had disgraced the Family.

On the 16th of May, 1974, we were given one-way tickets to Göteberg, Sweden.

11
Sweden, Norway, and Rubella

Give us your tired, your poor, your huddled masses, I thought silently, *and we will lift for you the liberating words of Moses David.* As we disembarked at the city of Göteborg, I felt a thrill of anticipation. Our failures were behind us. Perhaps, in this country, we could prove ourselves worthy of God's calling and bring enlightenment to the lost souls of Sweden.

But our exhilaration was short-lived. We found the colony housed in an apartment on the top floor of an ancient building off a secluded back street. The narrow winding stairs creaked as we mounted them, and we noticed that paint was flaking off the walls.

We knocked on the door to announce our arrival, only to be met with blank stares. No one had heard about any brethren coming from England.

We were admitted into the apartment with suspicion. There was always the possibility that we could be spies sent to infiltrate the ranks and glean information for anti-cult groups or desperate parents looking for their missing offspring. They would call the leadership to verify that we were authorized members of the Family.

Meanwhile; I wandered through rooms filled with beds piled high with backpacks and clothes. In a large, sunlit room littered with soiled diapers, I found a young woman bending over a baby.

"Hello, I'm Melita," I said loudly enough for her to

hear above the baby's cries.

She raised her head. "I'm Sarah." Her eyes dropped to my bulging figure. "I see you're pregnant," she observed.

"Yes," I said proudly. "Five months."

"Well, I hope you'll be happy here reaching Sweden for Moses David." She returned to the baby. There was an unmistakable note of sarcasm in her voice.

"Everything is okay," Seth called. "The leadership has confirmed that we're legit. Come on, Melita, let's put away our things and hit the streets."

Sarah and her American husband, Abraham, were the colony leaders. Abraham looked much like Jacob from London—the same small glasses, the same protruding teeth. He taught us some simple phrases to use when litnessing.

"Den har for du," he coached. *"Kan du hjalpa oss med liten pengar, vi, hjalpa narkotika.* This means, 'This is for you. Please help us with some spare change in our work with drug-addicts.' People are so 'sheepy' here, and so willing to give," he added. "Here, I'll write this phrase in Swedish on a card for you and you can show the card to people until you learn the words," he shot us a toothy grin.

So we made our first attempt to bring the word of Moses David to the people of Sweden. I stopped an older lady on the street, handed her a Mo letter, and showed her my card. She read the card and asked a question in Swedish. I shrugged my shoulders and looked innocent. She fumbled in her purse, muttering to herself, pressed a coin into my hand, and hurried on. I examined the coin. "50 oerer" was inscribed on it. At that time four Swedish crowns were worth approximately one dollar. Fifty oerer was half a crown, so my "generous" friend had given me the equivalent of 12½ cents. But I kept going. The more I smiled and flashed my little card, the larger the donations.

As the weeks rolled by, Seth and I grew accustomed to life in Sweden, Children of God style. We learned some basic vocabulary and became fond of Swedish meatballs and pancakes. But just as we were settling into the routine, we had to move on.

Word came that the colonies in Norway needed more laborers. In Oslo, we joined members of the Family who were camping on an island just outside the city. They had been trying to provision a house in Oslo for years, but so far "the Lord had provided" only the use of the island and some camping equipment. During the day a ferry boat made frequent trips between the island and the mainland.

We arrived on a cold, blustery day. The bitter sea wind stung our cheeks as we crossed the bay. On the island, we barely made it to a cluster of tents before the storm that had threatened on our brief voyage finally broke. The sky darkened and great, black clouds hurled icy pellets of rain and sleet. The women huddled inside one of the tents, while the men fought the furious weather to erect another tent. I worried that Seth would catch a cold because his only shoes were soaked through.

When the storm had subsided and colony life returned to normal, we met some of the brethren. The dominant, catalytic personality in the group was a thin, middle-aged American woman called Esther. Someone whispered confidentially that she had been the leader of the Jesus People Army in Seattle before she found a better way to serve the Lord.

She was gesturing wildly, flinging her arms into the air and shouting at the top of her lungs. Everyone sat spellbound, entranced by her dramatic oratory. It was clear by the reverent attitude of the listeners that she was considered to have prophetic powers.

Anah, a young Norwegian woman, who spoke fluent English, showed us our quarters. I looked apprehensively at what was to be my prenatal home—a tiny, two-man pup tent. How was I going to maneuver my now ballooning body in such cramped conditions? To live without proper bathroom facilities was bad enough, but to have to inch my way on my back into a pup tent seemed too much. Since I didn't want to appear to murmur against God's will, I suggested softly to Anah, "I'm going to have my baby soon. Do you think it would be possible for us to have a larger tent?"

"Can't you see how few tents there are?" she snapped impatiently.

I looked around. Two large tents formed the nucleus of the camp. These served as a meeting area by day, and segregated sleeping quarters for the single brothers and sisters by night. Another tent, which would sleep four people, was situated several yards away.

"Perhaps we could sleep in that smaller tent?" I mumbled.

"Definitely not! That's the leaders' tent."

Her menacing look stunned me into silence. I dared not suggest that my leaders be inconvenienced by the needs of a lowly disciple.

The weather grew warmer, and it was uncomfortable inside our stuffy tent. One of the sisters, noticing my discomfort, gave me a light, full-length cotton smock to replace my heavier winter clothing. But the long days of litnessing were hard and tiring. The sun was unbearably hot for one unaccustomed to such drastic changes in temperature.

At night I crawled into our tent, weary and ill. I lit a candle and lay beside Seth, listening to the sea crashing on the shore. The tent was our haven from the world—a harsh world where the dictates of domineering leaders crashed relentlessly upon broken lives. Here in our candlelit enclosure, at least we could take comfort in each other.

I tried desperately to deepen our communication.

"I'm frightened, Seth. I don't understand what's happening to me. I can't comprehend bringing a child into the world. Who is this person living inside me? I've fed and nourished this life for eight months now, yet I don't even know him."

Seth had no answers, but his arms were strong and secure. We were close during our time in the tent.

Morning always came and the sunlight invaded our private world, signaling another endless day of selling Mo letters under the hot sun. It was a rare treat to be allowed to go litnessing with Seth. Usually, I was paired with a younger brother or sister. Today it was young Joab of Greenwich Village.

As Joab and I got off the ferry boat, a summer storm broke. We waded through the wet, cobbled streets for hours, offering our literature and getting wetter by the second. My dress was soaked through and my flimsy sandals squeaked and oozed water as I walked. A fierce storm was also brewing within. If I continued litnessing in the rain, I would catch a chill; if I stopped litnessing to find shelter, I would be setting a poor example of faith before my younger brother. I was torn by doubt and bewilderment. I should have the faith to keep healthy. I should have the faith not to feel this conflict. *These are the thoughts of the Devil,* I decided. *I will refuse to acknowledge him as Mo has taught us.*

But I couldn't take it anymore. I told Joab that I needed some quiet time with the Lord and disappeared into the ladies' room in the art gallery.

As I entered the tastefully decorated restroom, prim and proper ladies looked disapprovingly at me. When I caught a glimpse of my reflection in the full-length mirror, I could understand their reaction. I looked dreadful. My hair hung in damp strings. My soggy dress clung to my huge figure. I looked like a waif, a tramp. Was this what my parents had raised me for? Could this possibly be God's will? Was this all life held?

I rushed into a stall and slammed the door behind me. I couldn't stop the tears. I cried for an hour or more, overwhelmed with feelings of desolation and frustration. Above all, I wanted to do God's will, but did He demand such a price?

When I finally emerged, Joab tactfully asked no questions. The rain had stopped. We spent a few more hours litnessing and then went to a meeting in the tiny city apartment where the top leadership lived.

As I listened to Esther's rousing exhortation, my spirits soared. Any sacrifice for the Lord would be rewarded mightily.

After the meeting Esther smiled at me, squeezed my arm affectionately and asked, "Melita, how are you? You are such a strong sister. God bless you and the fighting mothers of the Revolution."

"I'm fine, Esther. Praise the Lord!"

"Good, good. Praise God!" she said and squeezed my arm again.

"But there is something that's bothering me, Esther . . . something I'd like you to see. I'm not sure what it is . . ."

"Oh? Show me, dear."

"These spots on my stomach. Do you know what they are?" I showed her the sprinkling of red spots I had just discovered.

Her face grew serious. She motioned for some other leaders to come take a look.

"Those spots look serious, Melita."

In a rare display of concern, the leaders called a doctor who diagnosed the spots as rubella, a childhood disease that is serious only in the first three months of pregnancy. It was decided that I should remain with them until I was better. Though I joined in the prayers for a speedy recovery, I secretly reveled in the luxury of a real bed and some precious time of my own.

During the days, I napped, read, and visited with Charity, the "regional mother" in charge of the food, families, and pregnant women in the communes of Norway, who came to visit me often. I liked Charity. She, like most of the leadership, was American. She was small and wiry, with long, unkempt dark hair, glasses, and protruding teeth. Her friendly personality more than compensated for her plain features. We laughed and joked and talked about many things. The Mo letters were forgotten for the moment.

"Charity, you've had two children. What's it like? Does it hurt?" I asked.

She answered slowly and thoughtfully, "Melita, children and childbirth are blessings from God. Yes, it does hurt—somewhat. Here in the Family we don't believe in taking drugs during childbirth; we prefer to have our babies naturally. Just trust in the Lord and don't be afraid."

She fished around in her bag and produced a small black paperback book which she handed to me.

"Read this and give it back to me when you are finished. This book tells how to make childbirth easier. The Lamaze method consists mainly of breathing exercises which will help you take your mind off the pain."

I read the book and faithfully practiced the exercises, until I became adept at relaxing and concentrating on my breathing.

"Charity," I ventured one day, "what is the Family's attitude toward having babies in the hospital?"

"In the early days in the colonies the girls always had their babies at home." Charity launched into one of her favorite topics. "In the Mo letter *Faith and Healing*, Mo specifically encourages home deliveries. He says if your faith is strong enough, God will see you safely through. But things have changed. It's now acceptable to go to a hospital if you pray that God will protect you from the satanic spirits."

I grimaced. I didn't dare ask her about some of the dark rumors in circulation—that in one colony a baby had been born prematurely and the parents, trying to prove their faith, didn't take the baby to the hospital. The baby died. I didn't ask because it was unrevolutionary to ask questions. I could but wait and hope that, when my time came, God would forgive me for choosing to have my baby in an evil hospital.

12
The
Birth

My day to deliver was fast approaching, and as there was no place for us in Oslo, Seth and I were sent to Stockholm. The Family there had a big house in the suburb of Huddinge. We were told that a married couple was needed to shepherd the new training center in Stockholm, and Seth and I seized the opportunity because we were eager to prove ourselves as leaders.

Life in the comfortable Stockholm colony was a welcome change from the stony-floored, ant-infested tent. The Family had been given the use of a house in the suburbs. The basement was being finished with two additional bedrooms, a bathroom, and a living area. This was to be the "babes' ranch," the colony of young trainees that Seth and I would teach to become true revolutionaries.

The upstairs was reserved for leaders. Esther and her Danish husband, Valiant, came often to visit and were treated royally. Luke and Hope, as the resident leaders, oversaw the litnessing colony in the heart of Stockholm and other colonies in neighboring cities.

Seth and I were given a small converted hallway with a large adjoining room that was furnished as a nursery. I busied myself preparing for birth, collecting baby clothes and other items, and practicing my breathing techniques.

Often, when Seth was downstairs helping the

brothers finish the basement, I could sneak a snack and take a glorious afternoon nap. Hope, a petite, dark-haired American with the enthusiasm and vigor of a firebomb, took me under her wing. She had a baby whom she left in the care of others most of the time. Though her child cried incessantly, I regarded her as an authority on childbirth and child care. She encouraged me to practice my deep breathing exercises and she helped me to find a free prenatal clinic at the hospital.

By early September the "babes' ranch" in the basement was completed. The brothers had put in a shower, built two new bedrooms, and painted and carpeted throughout. We praised the Lord for His generous bounty in providing us with bunk beds, mattresses, carpeting, paint, and furniture, all donated by "interested businessmen."

Seth was to be the shepherd, responsible for training fifteen new disciples. Michael, a pushy Swede, was to be his top man, his undershepherd. He was sly, always on the lookout for opportunities to usurp Seth's authority.

Luke, Hope's smart-mouthed American husband, was the leader over all of us. He was to train us as babe-ranch shepherds in how to become competent brainwashers and indoctrinators.

"Repetition," urged Luke, "is the secret of memory. Keep filling their memory banks with the cleansing water of Mo's word. While their minds are being filled, they are also being washed from the filth of the world and their lukewarm church religion. Invest yourselves completely in these fifteen babes, and you will turn out fifteen soldiers to win Sweden and the world."

We worked out a rigorous schedule of Mo studies, Bible classes, and litnessing. We gave our charges twenty minutes of "free time" in the morning, but we expected that time to be spent in memorizing their Bible verses and Mo quotes for the day. Early in the morning and late at night, they listened to tape recordings of Mo letters and Bible readings. They must not have any time to think or listen to the Devil. Babes straight from the world are especially vulnerable.

We were ready for them. Fifteen eager-eyed babes moved in. No one looked older than twenty-three. Most of them were Swedish—a home-grown crop. Docilely, they submitted to our regimen and obeyed our commands. That is, everyone except Thamar.

Thamar was a heavy, dark-haired Swedish girl, with dark flashing eyes and a strong face. She was a tinder box—waiting to erupt at the slightest provocation. The problem was that not only were her parents antagonistic toward our Family, but Thamar would not submit her mind and will to us. Stubbornly and tenaciously she clung to her own ideas. She wouldn't let Mo, through his letters, do her thinking for her. She constantly told Seth how to run the colony and asked embarrassing questions about the Comet Kohoutek scare that had fizzled out. She was a bad influence on the rest of the sheep. Others began to raise questions and doubts. Something had to be done. We went to Luke with the problem.

"She's a hard case all right," said Luke, thoughtfully drumming his long bony fingers on the table. "She's headstrong and stubborn, but if you can break her and channel that energy into the Lord's work, she can be a dynamic sister."

We conferred often about which method would be most effective to break her will. We could send her on a long faith trip. Or we could call her up for a session of verbal discipline. But she might answer back. No, Thamar's case required a very subtle approach.

I had a special interest in this affair. In Thamar I saw a reflection of the girl I used to be—the once proud, independent spirit with the courage to defy tradition and set out in quest of truth. Now I despised her for these very qualities.

After we had prayed, I voiced an idea that came "from the Lord." Since Thamar was so cocky and sure of herself, we would give her a job certain to undermine her confidence. Kitchen duty was a menial task with endless complications. Planning and preparing food for both the babes and the leaders, keeping up with required studies, and being subject to humiliation when she made mistakes would certainly overwhelm her.

I wanted to break her as I had been broken, and in time she did break. The pressure of the job, the intensive indoctrination, the guilt and fear all undermined her sense of self; she became a mindless sheep like the rest of them.

As I neared full term, and it was harder to get around, I was allowed to rest in our room most of the day. Since Seth and I had attained the status of leaders, we were no longer required to do as much litnessing.

My predicted date of delivery came and went. I watched impatiently as the dates on the milk cartons changed. One week overdue, two weeks, three weeks. *Maybe I'll never go into labor*, I thought to myself glumly.

But, as I waddled upstairs with a glass of milk from the carton dated the 19th of September, I felt the first twinge of pain. As I eased myself into the chair to type some shepherd reports, I felt another. When they started to come every quarter of an hour, I sounded the alarm.

Hope and Seth rushed me downstairs and laid me on the bed. When my body began to tense with pain, Hope advised me it was time to concentrate on my breathing and relax. They left me alone and I could hear them talking quietly outside the door.

"It's just the beginning, Seth," Hope was saying. "It's only seven o'clock. This could go on all night. Put on a Mo letter tape for her and get on with your shepherd's report. Check on her regularly and, when it's time to go to the hospital, call me." Hope's calm manner was reassuring.

I played the tape over and over again, trying to concentrate on the words. But the contractions were becoming too intense and painful. I was frightened. I headed for the kitchen and the comfort of human companionship, stopping several times on the way for another contraction.

In the kitchen, Phoebe, a tiny Swedish sister, was playing secretary to Seth as he wrote the weekly shepherd's report. Seth pulled up a chair for me and started to tell amusing stories to get my mind off the pain. It was twelve o'clock. I had been in labor for five hours. I realized it was no use fighting the pain, hoping it would stop, or trying to run away. It had to be endured, conquered.

I followed the suggestions in the Lamaze book and fixed my eyes on a single flower in the lampshade which hung over the table. For the next eight hours, I concentrated on that flower. The time between contractions quickly decreased from fifteen minutes to two. At the first twinge of pain, I concentrated on my flower and began to breathe deeply. Finally, all I could do was wait and catch the next wave and ride it until it crashed. Once I missed my cue and the pain crept up on me, twisting me in its grasp before I could catch my breath and concentrate. I panicked and struggled wildly to shift my consciousness from the unbearable pain to the harmless flower on the shade.

Morning broke. Sunlight filtered through the curtains. It was time to go to the hospital, but no one would believe me.

"It's time! I know it's time!" I pleaded.

"Oh, just wait a little longer. The Lord will show us when to go."

"It's time to go now," I screamed tearfully. "Please take me now, Seth."

We made it to the hospital none too soon. I was rushed almost immediately into the delivery room. Seth and Hope were allowed to come with me.

Hope took my hand. I concentrated on her incredibly deep blue eyes, and followed her directions, "Breathe in . . . breathe out . . ."

On the periphery of my consciousness, I could sense confusion. Doctors were clocking my contractions, shaking their heads, and babbling in Swedish. They listened to the baby's heartbeat and shook their heads again. Then I saw one of them approaching me with surgical scissors.

"No, no, please don't cut me," I pleaded.

Hope explained in Swedish, "She wants to have her baby naturally, by trusting God."

The doctor turned to me, his face deadly serious and said, "Your baby could die if we do not perform an episiotomy. The umbilical cord is wrapped around the neck of the fetus, and the heartbeat is slowing down. If we wait, the child will die by strangulation."

And so, the cut was made—almost certainly saving my baby's life.

If I had had the "faith" to have my baby at home . . . No, I mustn't think thoughts like that. It's sinful and unrevolutionary. I must concentrate on bringing this baby safely into the world.

Seconds later, a tiny, red, wrinkled bit of humanity was placed on my stomach for my inspection—a healthy boy. My son. He was screaming lustily in protest of his unceremonious departure from the safety of his dark cocoon.

I endured the stitches that followed without drugs or painkillers. At least I could have that much faith. I quoted the Psalms at the top of my lungs with Seth and Hope while the doctor performed his needlework sans anesthesia.

We were congratulated with smiles of approval. I was assured that I had performed admirably and basked in the praise.

When one of the doctors came in to check me later, he asked, in his broken English, "How does it feel to be a mother?" I liked him, he had a kind face, and he had saved my son's life by insisting on the surgical procedure.

"I don't know," I replied truthfully.

"Yes, that is a very fine answer," he nodded. "Maybe I should wait and ask you again in a few years. Then you will know."

The nurses took time to show me how to breast-feed. When I finally summoned the courage to hold the warm, blanketed bundle in my arms, I felt a faint stirring, like the flutter of a butterfly's wing. I did not then recognize it as the maternal love that was to grow until it superseded all ties to the Family and Moses David.

That night I put on some slim red slacks and a bright top, tied back my hair and took my new son home—home to conquer postpartum depression and to survive the power struggle that was raging between Seth and Michael.

13
God Bless You – – And Get Out!

"Sister, you'd better get in the Spirit—and quick! Quit sniveling and pull yourself together!"

Before I could beg Seth to stay and help me with the baby, he was out the door. I knelt beside our bed and prayed for strength to make it through that day—and all the ones that followed in dismal succession.

I learned how to bundle the baby against the cold and strap him to my body for litnessing trips. Except for the feeding and diapering stops, I could litness as well as any other sister.

But while I was getting myself together, our babes' ranch was falling apart. The power struggle between Seth and Michael, coupled with Seth's lack of leadership ability, was destroying the ranch. Once again, Seth and I were relieved of our duties as leaders and sent elsewhere—to the litnessing colony, to the farm colony, on the road—anywhere to keep us out of the way and to avoid giving us responsibilities. After six months, we were back in Göteborg, Sweden, where we had started our Swedish ministry—and I was pregnant again.

During the months of change, endless moves, and adjustment to baby John, our marital relationship had been crumbling. Disagreements sprang up over every little thing, but John was usually the focal point. It began when Seth studied the Family child care letters.

"Melita," he said, "John is nearly ten months old. He needs to know what discipline means. The child care letters are very clear. When John does something wrong, we must tell him no. If he keeps doing it, we should count to three firmly and loudly. By the count of three, if he hasn't stopped, we should spank him. Then, if he cries, we should spank him until he stops crying. But always be sure to give him a chance to pray and repent afterward."

I was appalled. John was sitting in his buggy, playing with his pacifier—defenseless and innocent.

"But, Seth," I protested, "John is just a baby. He's too young to understand the one-two-three method of discipline. He isn't even walking or talking yet!"

"You're just like all women, Melita—soft! Mo says that children raised by women alone are spoiled brats. That's why the father has to be the disciplinarian. And I am going to discipline John as I see fit."

I didn't dare challenge the teachings of Mo or Seth's authority. To do so would be spiritual suicide. Instead, I tried to hush little John whenever he cried.

Other mothers were not so "soft." One day I picked up the sound of a child crying in the bathroom. It was Peter, a year-old toddler. His mother, Starlight, followed the child care letters strictly. The howls from the bathroom told me he had "disobeyed" and was receiving punishment. I wondered what minor infraction of her rigid rules he had committed now.

I could hear plainly what was going on behind the closed door.

"Peter, stop crying. Do you want to pray with me and ask Jesus to forgive you for being bad?"

No answer from Peter. Just howls and sobs. For thirty minutes it continued—a heavy hand on bare flesh . . . more entreaties from Starlight . . . screams of an hysterical child.

"Peter, stop crying or I'll have to spank you again. Stop it . . . stop it! All right—one, two, three . . ."

Finally there was silence. Maybe little Peter just fell asleep from sheer exhaustion. Starlight was not guilty of child abuse, by the standards of the Family. She was only following the revolutionary rules for training children to be good soldiers of Jesus and Moses David. One child care letter did warn that if a child required fifteen to thirty spankings in a week, he had a serious problem.

The bitterly cold Swedish winter brought new complications. Litnessing was hampered by snow-covered streets and we were forced indoors to witness to apartment-dwellers.

Our marriage was deteriorating rapidly now, affected by the weather, the dreary living conditions, and the continuing disagreements over little John's discipline. Then Jeremiah, our leader, dropped his bombshell.

"Melita," he approached me one day, "you know that a woman is physically subservient to the man, but it appears that you're the strong spiritual partner in your marriage. Esther and I have been praying seriously about your situation with Seth, and Esther has had a prophetic dream. She feels you're one of God's chosen people. She feels you're destined for great things in the Revolution."

"And Seth?"

"Seth wasn't in the dream. In fact, the Lord has told us that you shouldn't remain married to him. Seth isn't pulling his weight. He's holding you back. You'll have to separate, Melita."

"But . . ." I groped for words. "What about the baby I'm expecting and little John? He's not a year old yet and he needs his daddy."

"Where God guides, he provides," Jeremiah quoted glibly. "God will take care of you and the children. You will be sent to Stockholm to be trained as a layout artist for our printing operation there. Seth will be going to a farm with one or two other spiritually weak and dying brothers. Tomorrow you will go your separate ways. You are not to communicate with him. You are not to think about him again."

I was aghast—in shock from the impact of his words. When he signaled that I was dismissed, I obeyed meekly. No further questions.

The next morning, I watched Seth walk out of my life. As I stood at the corner with our unborn child kicking in my stomach, I watched until he disappeared into the maze of winding streets. Then he was gone. I went around to the back of the apartment building, hid behind the garbage dumpsters and cried. When I went back inside, my tears were dry.

A Swedish brother and sister met me at the train station in Stockholm. The colony was housed on the sixth floor of an ancient apartment building on one of the main streets. I dragged myself and my born and unborn children up the flights of stairs, hoping that someone would help me with the buggy. But no one came.

"Please, God," I prayed, "don't let them send me out litnessing. Touch their hearts to let me rest. I'm about to drop from exhaustion."

Two pregnancies in quick succession, combined with the emotional stress and physical hardship of our sudden separation from Seth had taken their toll on me. I was worn out and depressed. I cried whenever I was alone and prayed that God, in His infinite mercy, would give me back my husband.

But the colony leader was an energetic young Swede who didn't understand that the baby woke promptly at five each morning to be fed and that I badly needed rest by afternoon. His colony was running low on funds, so his demands were merciless. "Get out and get litnessing!"

Day after day I dragged myself through the streets, pushing the buggy and the Mo letters, and returning to the colony to fall into bed. One evening I found the Family buzzing with activity. Mo's son-in-law and some other high-ranking officials were expected for a conference that was to last a week or more. All the disciples would have to hit the road to make room for them.

"Hit the road?" I gasped. "But John is just a baby and I'm five months pregnant!"

"Doubts, doubts, doubts, Melita. When will you ever learn to have faith that God will provide?" the leader said in an annoyed manner. "Two of the new babes will go with you. You'll be all right."

I slowly gathered our things and packed them in the buggy. At the door, the leader instructed me to telephone each evening to report our litnessing statistics and receive new orders.

"God bless you, Brother and Sisters. Shine for Jesus!" he said, and shut the door in our faces.

The babes in my care were of no more help than little John. They were tinder boxes of trouble—full of doubts and complaints. It was up to me, I found, to bring in enough money to feed the four of us with enough left over to turn in to the colony leader.

One morning, after litnessing for several hours, I left the two babes to find a cheap café. It was time for John to eat and I was weak with hunger. On a narrow side street, I found a likely-looking place. As I strapped John into the high chair, I scanned the menu, and ordered an inexpensive item. We ate with relish, then went into the restroom to change John's diaper. When I returned, the bill was waiting for me. It came to nine crowns. I counted my money. Only seven crowns! It couldn't be true. I counted again, then rummaged through my pockets and purse. Nothing. The proprietress stood behind the cash register, waiting. I bowed my head on the table and began to sob. Never had I felt so alone and forsaken.

The kindly proprietress came to inquire about my problem. In broken Swedish, I explained my predicament. When she understood what I was saying, her face creased in a sympathetic smile.

"Don't worry, my child," she said slowly in English. "Just give me the money you have and that will be enough. Let me fill the baby's bottle for you."

This unexpected display of kindness brought forth another torrent of tears. Her understanding attitude was in sharp contrast to the hostility and sneers I encountered on the streets all day and the insensitivity of my leaders.

"Thank you," I said as I dried my eyes and handed her the bottle. "God bless you. You're very kind. When I get the two crowns, I'll come back and pay you."

"No, no, dear. Keep your crowns for yourself and your babies." She patted John's curly head as he gurgled in delight.

Gathering all the fortitude I could muster, I hit the streets again. But no one wanted Mo letters. When I stopped to check with my two partners, I found that their day had gone as badly as mine.

"Well, praise the Lord!" I said with forced enthusiasm. "When the going gets tough, the tough get going. Let's just keep on trying to be good soldiers for Jesus and mighty men for Moses David."

The grey afternoon wore and John began to fret and cry. I tried to interest him in his toys, but he wouldn't be pacified. He wanted out of his buggy, but I couldn't stop. I hadn't sold enough Mo letters and if I didn't reach my quota by the time I phoned in, I would be rebuked and we would go hungry for dinner.

Day after day, John fussed and cried. Concerned middle-aged matrons glared their disapproval.

As night fell, the twinkling lights transformed Stockholm into a magical city. People in evening attire hurried by on their way to various entertainment spots. No one had time for a pregnant Irish girl peddling religious literature.

The disapproving matrons were all at home, tucked into their warm beds. And now the pleasure-seekers of the night stared curiously at me and my baby buggy.

"Sir, would you like to buy one of these? We are a Christian group helping drug addicts."

The well-dressed Swede paused, saw the desperation on my face, and pressed a ten-crown note into my hand. At least we were assured of breakfast, but there was still no place to sleep.

As we waited, I repeated a verse of Scripture: "Rejoicing in hope; patient in tribulation; continuing instant in prayer" (Rom. 12: 12). I drew some comfort from this verse. I was enduring patiently the hardships I believed God was placing in my life. And I was praying continually that God would bring Seth back to me.

When John became ill, I put in a desperate call to the shepherd, intercepted by his secretary. "Please let us come in. My baby is sick and I have not sold a single letter today. There is no money for food."

The answer was firm. "Be grateful the Lord is testing your faith so you can learn to trust in Him for all things."

Without permission, I took refuge in the hallway of the apartment building where the Family occupied the top floor. I sat on the cold stone steps, rocking the buggy while John slept. Secretly I hoped that a member of the Family would see our plight and take pity on us.

Though two or three leaders passed by with a casual "God bless you," they didn't offer to take us in. I could smell the rich aroma drifting from the apartment and could imagine the sumptuous meal prepared for the leaders—a smorgasbord of cheeses, meats, pickles, caviar, and an assortment of breads, yogurt, and fruit. I tried to suppress my envy. We had been taught that our leaders deserved twice as much consideration because of their grave spiritual responsibility.

Sitting there, miserable and hungry, I allowed my

mind to wander. Perhaps the leaders really didn't care about us at all, for all their pious talk about love. If they did, they surely would not have let me go hungry on the streets with a sick baby and no place to go.

I was frightened by these seditious thoughts, but even more concerned for our survival. I prayed for forgiveness for what I was about to do, then went to a phone booth and placed another call.

This time I asked to speak directly to one of the leaders. Again, the secretary refused to "disturb their conference," but agreed to take the message.

"Tell them," I said, "that we've been living on the road for over a week. John is sick and I'm nearly six months pregnant. Tell them we are having trouble raising funds and finding places to sleep at night. Tell them I'm coming in."

To my surprise the leaders received me cordially, almost apologetically. Arrangements had been made for us to move to a suburban colony where Seth would rejoin us within a few days. Much later I learned that there had been big trouble at the leadership conference. A key issue, it seemed, was an investigation by the Swedish police into alleged reports of young, pregnant women with babies—roaming the streets at night . . .

My ecstatic reunion with Seth was short-lived. Soon after the three of us were together again, an old scene was replayed.

The first rays of sunlight filtered through the thin curtains of our bedroom and into John's crib, stirring him from sleep. John's first thoughts were for food and companionship. "Wha!" His wail brought Seth to his feet, grumbling at this early disturbance. He settled John back in his bed, covered him with his blanket, and told him to go back to sleep.

John stared at Seth with uncomprehending, baby eyes. His lip quivered and he began to cry. Seth's repeated commands to go back to sleep went unheeded as John continued howling. He wanted up. He wanted food. He wanted companionship.

"Oh, Seth, let him up," I said as I struggled out of bed. "I'll get him a bottle. He always wakes up at this time of morning. He won't go back to sleep now."

"No, Melita, he has to learn to obey," Seth insisted stubbornly. "If he doesn't stop crying by the time I count to three, I'm going to spank him."

"Please don't, Seth," I gasped in horror. "He's only a baby. You can't spank a baby."

"He's not a baby anymore. We don't have babies in the Revolution; we have little people. And John needs to be disciplined. As head of this household, I intend to see that he is!" He turned to John who was crying even more loudly.

"John, stop crying right now . . . One . . . Two . . . Three . . ." he counted. John didn't stop crying. Seth snatched the alarmed baby from his crib, pulled down his diaper and administered several heavy smacks.

But the child care "formula" didn't work. And I stood helplessly by, John's cries tearing me apart.

I was saved, at least temporarily, from this torture by new orders from our leaders. As the first chill of winter bit the air, we said goodbye to Sweden and boarded the boat for . . .

14
And the Walls Came Tumbling Down

Dublin . . . my home! The pale morning light crept over the bay as our boat docked. As we made our way through the familiar, cobbled streets, a curious comfort stole over me. I was in my own land, among people whose language and culture I understood. I could reach out and touch my roots. The steerage pattern was reversed. I had left Ireland in hope of a better life. Now I had returned—with the same hope. Here, we could follow God and Moses David without the burden of pompous leadership. Here, I could have my baby—the baby that I would not allow Seth or anyone else to take from me. With this baby I would prove that I was a competent mother.

We spent the day settling into our new quarters on the outskirts of town. But at the first opportunity, I hurried into downtown Dublin, hungry for the sight of familiar landmarks. There was picturesque Saint Stephan's Green and fashionable Grafton Street; the department store where my mother had purchased most of my childhood clothes and toys and the cheap café where the drug freaks had hung out when I was a young teenager; there was a strange mixture of bustling street traffic next to the serene campus of historic old Trinity College.

Then there was Richard . . . Seth's brother arrived from America one busy morning in January. I was surprised to find him looking much younger than his thirty years. He wore a sailor cap, and his youthful face was constantly creased in a broad, boyish grin.

"How are you doing, Brother?" he said, slapping Seth on the back. "And hello, Sister-in-law. I'm very, very pleased to meet you, ma'am," he greeted me in his charming American drawl. "You're a true Irish colleen." His gaze was openly admiring.

While I prepared dinner, Seth talked with Rich and played some Family albums for him. After dinner and light conversation, Seth and I moved in our our main objective—to convert Richard to the Children of God.

"Rich, would you like to read the Bible with me?" I invited. "There is a passage here that I think would help you understand why Seth and I have chosen to live with the Family. It's in Luke 14:33: 'He . . . that forsaketh not all that he hath, . . . cannot be my disciple,' and in Mark 16:15, 'Go ye into all the world, and preach the gospel to every creature.' The Children of God are among a very few Christians in the world who have been willing to forsake everything and follow God—not just try to buy him off with some change in the offering plate on Sunday morning."

"Yeah, Melita, I understand what you're saying. But I believe I serve God in my own way. And what about the good Christian people in America?"

"What 'good Christian people?'" I retorted. "The people who truly love Jesus are following Moses David, God's anointed endtime prophet. The so-called Christians in America are self-righteous Pharisees. God has given us direct prophecy that He is going to punish America for turning away from Him. So Moses David has told us to flee the ungodly American system before its destruction, which is coming very soon—and to warn others to do the same."

Rich still wasn't convinced. Disgusted, he returned to

America before we could persuade him to reconsider. But we continued to pray for his conversion to the Family.

Shortly before the baby's birth, the political conditions in Ireland worsened. Evidence of IRA terrorism was everywhere. Bombs were planted in boxes and between draperies in department stores. The evacuation of stores was commonplace.

It was during the height of the political tension that a sister reported a strange occurrence while she was litnessing. A shady-looking character had approached her on the street and told her that he knew her legal name and the address of her mother.

"I'm from the IRA," he said, "We're watching you closely."

We were panic-stricken. The terrorists, the kneecap-shooters, the finger-breakers were watching us! Through we could never verify the identity of the stranger, his knowledge of our members and their activities was alarming. This triggered a reaction of fear which facilitated the next major policy change.

An edict was handed down that the British Isles, like America, had rejected God's prophet, Moses David, and would have to suffer His wrath. It was time for us to flee "like a bird to your mountain"—to leave the wicked islands to their sure destruction.

Members of the Family began to see visions and receive prophecies. It was becoming apparent that God was moving to colonize "the uttermost parts of the world." Many were trying to raise money for their fare to India and other countries. Because of my approaching delivery, Seth and I stayed behind to close up the colony.

Michael was born at 7:30 A.M. after a long labor—without drugs and without Seth's comforting presence. Husbands were not allowed in the delivery room.

As the baby was placed in my arms, he stopped crying and stared intensely into my face, as curious about me as I was about him.

Now you're mine, little one, I thought, *really mine. I'm not going to let the Family and your father take you away from me. I don't care what the child care letters say! Nothing is going to separate us.*

We arrived in the colony at Liverpool at the beginning of a hot summer. There was much enthusiasm among the Family members who were preparing to leave for foreign mission fields.

In the midst of all the confusion, we met Gideon, the shepherd. Gideon was small and bespectacled—generally friendly and personable, but with rare, black moods when he could swoop down like a vulture and wound with his caustic tongue. He was a curious mixture—a musician whose artistry could transform us to lofty heights and a prophet whose exhortations were sprinkled with crude remarks and off-color jokes. He boasted incessantly of his sexual prowess.

I got the distinct impression that Gideon was leading us inexorably toward a day when all the walls of decency and propriety would come tumbling down.

But by the end of the summer we, too, obeyed Moses' evacuation plan for the British Isles and returned to Sweden.

15
Flirty Fishing

"When you go into the nightclubs and discos, be prepared to go to bed with anyone you meet—anyone. Every lost sheep deserves to be *shown* the love of God," thundered Isaac, our shepherd, quoting from a recent Mo letter, instructing the Family in the art of Flirty Fishing.

"'Inasmuch as ye have done it unto one of the least of these my brethren, ye have done it unto me' (Matt. 25:40). That also means," he interpreted, "that if you withhold physical love from even the most undesirable brother or sister, you are withholding love from God Himself!'"

We were expected to be love-slaves, toiling on the Scandinavian streets, returning home only to receive more instructions. Night after night we heard our leader reading statements justifying Moses David's incredible new doctrines.

"Don't worry about contracting a social disease or getting pregnant. God will give you the grace to endure. Besides, we need more babies for the Revolution. Love babies for Jesus! Hallelujah!" Isaac cried, his round face feverish with excitement.

"God is love," he continued, "and the Bible says, 'There is no law against love.' We are showing these poor lost souls the love of God when we are fulfilling their sexual needs. The church-going, self-righteous hypocrites would shudder at that, wouldn't they? But there is nothing evil or sinful about anything created by God. These churchy Systemites say we are sinning, that we are committing fornication and adultery. But they are lying! Remember, what the world thinks of us is not important!

"So what if we are called prostitutes? Jesus was also attacked by His enemies. He was called a glutton, a winebibber, a companion of harlots and radicals. We know He was none of those things. Nor are we prostitutes. We accept money only to further the work of the Lord—to save the world from eternal damnation!" Isaac's voice rose dramatically as he paused, giving us time to absorb the full impact of his words.

Despite these nightly sermons, I couldn't accept the fact that God really expected *me* to become a "hooker for Jesus." I was a respectable wife and mother. Surely, only the unmarried sisters would be required to perform these services. My mind recoiled in horror. Nevertheless, when I walked downtown to peddle Mo letters, my cheeks burned with shame. Though I was innocent, I imagined everyone must know about the new directives and that I, too, was branded one of "God's harlots."

More and more often, as I sold literature from door to door in apartment buildings, I found myself peering longingly inside, wishing I had a place of my own where my children and I could live normally.

"Seth, it's a long distance telephone call for you," called out Praise, Isaac's new wife.

"It must be Richard," said Seth. "He wrote that he might visit us again."

They talked on the phone for a long time. I could hear laughter and joking coming from the room.

"Richard wants to see us," announced Seth, as he strode into our bedroom. "And I don't know if that's such a good idea, Melita. His visit will take precious

litnessing time. He is such a spiritually weak brother. I
don't know if he'll ever join the Revolution. He has
taken drugs for so long, and now that his wife has left
him, he's pretty upset."

"Poor guy. He sounds like he really needs the Word.
If he came to visit us, that would give us a chance to
help him," I suggested. "I believe Rich really loves the
Lord. He just needs to be guided into the right way to
serve Him."

We discussed Richard for hours: his problem with
drugs, his emotional instability, his wife's desertion.
Seth suggested maybe I should go to bed with him in
order to recruit him for the Family. I laughed nervously
at the suggestion. Although Flirty Fishing was now in
operation in other colonies throughout the Family, our
colony had not yet adopted the practice.

But before Richard could pay us his promised visit,
we were uprooted once again. Since our Swedish visas
were running out and the authorities were reluctant to
renew them, our leaders decided that we should go to a
colony in a remote corner of northern Norway.

We traveled to the city of Trondheim by train to join
another revolutionary couple in an antiquated apartment over a junk shop.

Shiloah was an "older" member of the Family. Any
member over forty who had not made it to a top leadership position was eyed with suspicion. Shiloah was one
of these older men; he wore faded jeans and tattered
cord jackets and tried to affect the enthusiasm of an
adolescent. His wife, Rachel, was a bright and bouncy
college dropout who would have been pretty were it not
for her mouthful of crooked teeth. She often laughed
loudly and gaily.

Shiloah and Rachel had just had their second baby, a
girl. We two couples, together with our four children,
made up the entire colony, where Shiloah was the
leader by virtue of his age and rank. He was often ar-

rogant and abrupt in his commands, with a compulsive need to exert his authority. I supposed it was to compensate for his lowly place in the Family.

In our cramped apartment a familiarity developed among the four of us that began to ferment into smoldering resentment. Though Seth and I could physically retreat into our bedroom, there was no mental, spiritual, or emotional privacy. Everything was subject to the rule of Shiloah—the colony king.

It was into this resentment-riddled atmosphere that the latest orders came from the supervising shepherds.

"This is heavy stuff," said Shiloah in his infuriatingly labored English. He fingered the coveted letter containing the orders while we waited in suspense. He opened the envelope slowly and deliberately, withdrew the letter and read silently, then lifted his eyes to our expectant faces.

"We are to begin the Flirty Fishing ministry in this part of Norway right away. We have delayed obeying the Lord too long. There are lost, hungry souls crying out to know the truth in discos and nightclubs all over town. We need to start visiting these places several times a week.

"One night Rachel and I can go and leave our children with you; the next night you two can go and we will look after your boys. Praise God! We are going to work together and win this town for Jesus! Amen!"

"Amen," we chorused weakly.

Upstairs in our bedroom, Michael started to cry. Shiloah nodded permission for me to leave. As I closed the door, I heard him saying that they were going to read the latest Mo letter.

I was relieved to have an excuse to slip away by myself. I must have time to think. If anyone asked why I took so long, I could always say I had had a hard time getting Michael back to sleep.

As I rocked the baby, I leafed absentmindedly

through the book of Mo letters dealing with sex.

Michael had begun to coo, staring wide-eyed at the ceiling, when I stumbled across part of a Mo letter that had the effect of a mild thunderbolt. I gasped. I had read the letter before, but somehow I had never absorbed its real meaning. Now the meaning stood out all too clearly: Moses David advocated child sex! I read on quickly. Not only did he sanction sexual activity between children, boasting of his own early explorations and an aborted attempt at intercourse at age seven, but he also condoned relations between adults and children. He merrily recounted incidents where his babysitter had performed sexual acts on him as a child to put him to sleep.

My stomach churned.

Why hadn't I seen that before?

How many other obscenities had I been blind to?

I lifted my chubby-cheeked infant and held him close as his eyelids began to close. He curled up in the fetal position and smiled in his sleep, secure in the fact that his Mamma was here. I watched him as he slept and thought how Moses was encouraging us to abuse our children.

A painful stirring began in my brain. After five years of mindlessly following, obeying, and repressing my own thoughts, I began to think. I thought about Flirty Fishing, the sexual abuse of innocent children, Mo's harem of wives . . .

Downstairs I heard Seth calling me. I hurried to avoid angering him.

"Tomorrow we will begin our Flirty Fishing ministry," Shiloah was saying as I entered the room. "Praise God, Brethren!" he shouted. "We are going to get with it in this colony and obey God!"

Richard chose this difficult time for his visit. He had learned of our move to Norway and telephoned to ask us to meet his train.

As we waited, we litnessed in the station. We worked furiously to distribute our quota before Richard came.

A fascinating assortment of people passed through, on the way to their various destinations. Middle-aged businessmen, clutching their briefcases. Young travelers, weary under their heavy backpacks. Colorful Laplanders, conspicuous in their bright native dress and reindeer boots. All these people—yet not one wanted to buy a Mo letter!

I ran frantically from person to person, parroting one of the few Norwegian phrases I knew: "This is for you. Please read it and donate some money to our youth group. We help drug addicts." I seemed to be running headlong into a stone wall, a wall built of hostile, unsympathetic faces.

Mesmerized by the dizzying effect of my own words and the constantly shifting crowd, I began to panic. I experienced a lonely terror. I felt I was losing myself. Imprisoned by invisible bars, I longed to scream for help. But even the comfort of a common language was denied me. I was trapped.

I was at the mercy of a religious madman who wanted to control my mind and use my body for prostitution; who ruthlessly exploited my fear of the unknown, dangling it over my head like a sword suspended by the barest of threads; convincing me that those threads would snap if I became a dissenter.

"There he is now! There's Rich getting off the train," Seth's voice slowed my tumbling thoughts. "Come on! Let's go and greet him!"

"Hi there, brother Seth," grinned Rich.

He turned to me. "And Melita." He looked at me too intensely and hugged me too hard and too long. I stepped back, uncomfortably.

"Hi, Rich! God bless you!" I spoke quickly to cover my embarrassment. "Good to see you again. Did you have a nice trip?"

As we walked back to the colony, Rich chattered incessantly, directing most of the conversation to me.

We spent the rest of the day listening to Rich recount his adventures on the trip over. After dinner I could sense Seth's growing restlessness. I supposed he was feeling guilty because we were just sitting around making idle conversation.

When someone suggested that I take Rich to a disco, he was more than ready for some excitement. Seth gave me permission to go and took over the care of the children.

In the dimly lit disco, Rich told me about his heartbreak over his wife's leaving. I listened sympathetically and piously suggested that all his problems would be solved if he would only follow God and join the Family. Later, in the evening, he told me that his loneliness had driven him to cold, businesslike prostitutes. As the evening wore on, I felt his pain and longed to ease it if I could. Finally, in the strangely intimate atmosphere of the crowded discotheque, Rich told me he loved me.

That night Rich and I slept together—Rich, in his loneliness; I, in obedience to the Mo directive.

Rich was asking too many questions. He wanted to know where the money went that we sent every week to our leaders. He attacked the Flirty Fishing doctrine, although he had benefited from it. I, too, was filled with doubt over what we had done. I was not sure I could continue to Flirty Fish. He questioned Mo's relationship with the Libyan leader, Colonel Qadaffi, and was concerned over Mo's pro-Communist leanings. He questioned the right of the Family to break up my marriage to Seth when we were in Sweden.

"You know, Melita, there is something very wrong here. If you want to leave, I'll help you come to the States. Mom would love to have you and the kids."

"Thanks, Rich, but you're the one who needs to change." I laughed off his questions and accusations because I couldn't answer them. But his questions fueled my own intense desire to know the truth.

Then it was my turn to fish for strangers. Rich went along with Seth and me.

The small disco was crowded and hazy with smoke. The booths were filled to overflowing and couples danced closely on the dance floor. We sat down in a booth next to a young man and his girl friend.

Seth started a friendly conversation with the young man, a British disc jockey and his pretty girl friend.

"He's a sheep, Melita," Seth whispered in my ear. "Go after him."

This was the test of my obedience to Mo and of my love for the lost. I looked at my prospective Fish who turned back to make conversation with the girl.

"I can't do it," I told Seth.

I could see the anger flickering in his eyes.

"What do you mean you can't do it? What's the matter with you? He needs Jesus, can't you see that? Why don't you do as I tell you and as God tells you through Moses, and go after him?" Seth whispered hoarsely.

My reply was a look of defiance. I asked Rich to dance and left the booth. For the rest of the evening, I stayed close to him and avoided Seth and the Englishman. As long as I was with Rich, I was protected from Seth's fury.

On the way home I looked up at the stars twinkling chastely in the crisp, clear, northern night. Looking at them, I promised myself that if it was the last thing I ever did, I was going to leave the Family.

16
Breaking Point

In a Norwegian newspaper, nearly five years after my first encounter with the cult, I saw a picture of the man who had for so long controlled my thoughts, my feelings, my lifestyle—David Brandt Berg, alias Moses David.

I could not believe my eyes. This was not the dynamic, Christlike figure I had pictured. Instead, he was a caricature of the magnificent leader we had worshipped. He was old, wasted, and ugly! Sparse white hair hung limply to his shoulders and his long beard fell to his sunken chest. He sat, Buddha-like, with one hand resting on the leg of his chief wife. A bevy of scantily-clad women surrounded him, smiling seductively. Mo was eyeing them lustfully and his mouth was contorted in a sensual leer.

Was this grinning lecher the man to whom I had submitted my will—the man I had believed to be God's divine spokesman? As I studied the picture, I saw a reflection of myself. I was in him and he was in me. I was sickened! Over the years I had been deluded into submitting my mind to his perverted teachings and now he wanted to use my body as well!

I stood gazing at the picture in horror, then threw down the paper and fled to my room.

Rich had gone out with Shiloah and Rachel, leaving Seth and me to put the four children to bed. I didn't tell

Seth about my reaction to the picture. But I did tell him what I was planning.

"Seth, I've got to get away. I can't believe Flirty Fishing is God's idea. I want to leave the Family."

Seth flew into a rage and woke the baby. Afraid that he would strike me, I fled from the room and hid downstairs. Over Michael's wails, I could hear Seth alternately weeping and shouting. I waited until he calmed down, then slipped up the stairs to bed.

I was alone in the bedroom early the next morning when Rich burst in.

"Just what is going on here?" he demanded angrily. "When I went out with Shiloah and Rachel, she picked up a sailor in the bar. She just picked him up, Melita! Then Shiloah left her there with the guy!" He seemed incredulous. "Her baby has been crying for her all night. What is this garbage?" Rich didn't wait for a reply, but stalked out and slammed the door.

I dressed quickly and followed him, thinking I might be able to explain. But he continued his monologue.

"It's ridiculous, Melita," he said, staring through the skylight into the overcast morning sky. "The whole scene here is insane. A woman goes out to make some sailor happy and leaves her newborn baby to cry all night. You can't really believe that's right, can you, Melita?" His dark eyes searched my face.

Finally, all my dammed-up doubts and confusion broke through and tumbled out in a verbal torrent.

"Maybe you're right, Rich," I sobbed. "Maybe the Flirty Fishing is wrong. Maybe Moses and the whole Family are wrong—a huge, ghastly mistake. But I've believed in them for a quarter of my life. I want to leave, but I don't want to lose my soul or my heavenly rewards! I don't know what to do!"

"I know, I know," he comforted, "but you'll lose your sanity if you stay. Mom and I will help you and the children."

Suddenly, the outside world that I had been taught to regard as the Devil's domain, loomed like a great, dark chasm. In spite of what I had just learned about Moses David, I was terrified at the thought of leaving the familiar rituals of the Family. I stood teetering on the brink of decision.

"If I do leave, Rich, will you help me?" I begged desperately, clutching Rich's arm.

"Sure, Melita," he soothed. "I told you Mom and I will help."

With that small measure of security, I went downstairs to face the consequences of my decision.

Shiloah had already heard the news. "Seth tells me that you're thinking of leaving us, Melita." His face was difficult to read.

I took a deep breath. "Yes, I am, Shiloah."

"Perhaps, before you make such a life-changing decision, we'd better seek wisdom from God's Word."

We sat cross-legged in the living room, and opened our Bibles. Ironically, the passage Shiloah had selected followed the Beatitudes where Jesus clearly condemned sexual impurity. We read: "Thou shalt not commit adultery: But I say unto you, That whosoever looketh on a woman to lust after her hath committed adultery with her already in his heart" (Matt. 5:27–28).

"See here," cried Rich, waving his Bible in the air. "This verse proves that Firty Fishing is wrong. Christ says that adultery is a sin. Therefore, Flirty Fishing is a sin."

"But you've got to take that verse in context, Brother," said Rachel, her voice tinged with irritation. "The Bible says that "love is the fulfilling of the law" (Rom. 13:10), so if you show your love to someone through sex, it couldn't be a sin."

"Oh, yeah? What kind of loving mother would pick up a sailor and leave her baby to cry all night?" Rich retorted and left the house in disgust.

Shiloah's face had turned dark and threatening. His tone was measured. Every word left a burning brand emblazoned on my mind.

"You *do* remember the Bible's warning to those who leave God's true ways, don't you, Melita? 'Because they received not the love of the truth, . . . God shall send them strong delusion, that they should believe a lie: That they all might be damned who believed not the truth' (2 Thess. 2:11).

"You may leave, Melita, but you are leaving God's truth behind. As the Bible says, God will let you believe a lie because that's what you want. *You'll never know if you did the right thing.*"

So this was the Family's trump card—the ultimate psychological ploy to undermine my decision.

I was thoroughly frightened. I no longer knew what to believe. I didn't know if Moses and the Family were right or wrong. All I knew was I couldn't stay—not one minute longer than I had to.

I put through a collect call to my parents. When I heard my father's voice on the telephone, relief swept over me.

"Daddy . . . Hello, Daddy? I want to come home. The Children of God have gotten into prostitution, and I can't stay here any longer."

"I'm glad to hear that, Chick. When will you be arriving? Will Seth and the children be with you?"

"I'll be bringing the children with me, Daddy, but I don't know about Seth . . ."

"Mammy has your room ready as always." He sounded pleased. "Telephone me when you get to England. See you soon, Chick." And he hung up.

Relieved, I replaced the receiver, thanking God for parents who had always loved me even when they had not understood me.

When I went into the bedroom to pack, I was confronted by an irate husband.

"You're not taking the children with you, you know," he said. His tone was evil and menacing. "I will not allow them to be taken back into the sinful world. And you can also be sure we'll check through your belongings. You'd better not try to take any Mo letters with you." He spat out his words with contempt and hatred, then turned and disappeared down the stairs.

I sat, with the clothes half-folded in my lap. What should I do next? I certainly wasn't physically strong enough to fight him for the children? Was I going to be forced to leave them in this awful place?

When I rejoined the others, Seth greeted me in an almost civil manner.

"Melita, Honey," he began, "Shiloah and I have decided that I should go with you to London. Until the Lord opens your eyes to the truth, you need my protection." He tried to smile, but it more nearly resembled a sneer.

"Thank you, Seth." At least I wouldn't have to leave the children behind.

The finality of my decision gnawed uneasily at me as we loaded our belongings onto an old, wooden pushcart and moved them to the dock. I wasn't accustomed to making decisions on my own. *If I'm wrong*, I thought miserably, *and the Family really does have the truth as it claims, then I'm making the most serious mistake of my life.*

Rich brought our boat tickets to London and pressed them into my hand. "I want you to know," he said when we were out of Seth's hearing, "that I'm glad to help you out of this mess. Mom told me on the telephone this morning that she wants you all to come stay with her. Maybe if Seth could be around his own family for awhile, he would snap out of all this nonsense."

"Oh, Rich. I do want to get out of here, away from the

Family and, if possible, get Seth out, too."

"Then I'll help you with the fare and the visa. You'll need a sponsor."

I was touched by his eagerness to help us.

"I could never have faced the leaders or Seth alone. Thanks for all you have done. And starting over in the States sounds like a good idea."

The boat was ready to pull out of the harbor. We said hurried goodbyes. As we pulled away, I could see Rich above the crowd.

"See you in America," he called, with his face creased in its characteristic broad grin.

The trip to London was long and tedious. I had crossed that body of water too many times. I lay in my bunk and stared at the ceiling. I couldn't keep the tears back any longer. At this very moment, I was leaving the Family and, I believed, all my heavenly rewards. As the boat swayed gently, I knew I was embarking on another sort of journey—the longest and most difficult of all —the journey back to reality and life outside the Family.

17
The Journey Back

My parents stood waiting for us on the dark platform of the train station—my small, white-haired mother, clutching her purse; my father, standing tall beside her, anxiously scanning the crowd and checking his watch. Our train was late.

"Here we are!" cried my mother when she saw us. I ran to meet them. There were warm hugs, especially for the two grandchildren. Yet, despite our joyous reunion, there was tension within our little group. The conversation centered around trivialities and carefully avoided any mention of The Children of God and the real reason I was coming home.

"Una, dear, it's been so long since we've seen you and the boys. They've grown so. And you need some clothes, dear. Well, we can take care of that tomorrow . . ." she rambled as we drove home.

I chatted about the trip over, but soon lapsed into silence, leaving Seth to do all the talking.

The children had fallen asleep on our laps, exhausted from the long journey. I glanced out the window at the star-studded night and the familiar sights of London. A wave of relief swept over me. I was safe. I was home. The long arm of Moses David couldn't reach me here. I had taken the first step on the road back.

My attention shifted to Seth's idle conversation. He was joking as if everything were perfectly normal. My parents laughed politely. I looked into his vacant face and empty eyes and turned away in disgust. He seemed completely unconcerned about my mental anguish. I couldn't believe that he had grown so callous that he hadn't been appalled by the Family's prostitution and Moses David's child-sex directives. What kind of human being was he? Or had he become only a lifeless puppet, dangling from the strings of that monster, Moses David?

When the children were tucked in bed and Seth had settled down for the night, I slipped down to the kitchen where Daddy was brewing a cup of tea.

"What do you think of all this, Daddy?" I asked, leaning forward eagerly for his reply. His opinion was very important to me. At the moment, I could not think rationally; I could only feel.

"I think David Berg is insane," he answered without hesitation.

"And what about his new directive, 'Flirty Fishing,' religious prostitution?" I probed.

"It's white slavery. He can't get away with it much longer, Chick," he slapped the table emphatically. "I allowed you to join that group of fanatics, thinking you would get the whole business out of your system and be back home in a few weeks. But it got completely out of hand. Now it seems to be an international racket. You did the right thing coming home."

His forthright criticism of Moses David and the Family supported my own growing convictions. I needed the strength and wisdom of this man who had loved me all my life.

Later, as I snuggled between the crisp, clean sheets, gradually relaxing from our travels and the emotional trauma of the last few days, I heard John stirring uneasily in his sleep. Suddenly, he screamed and sat upright, crying uncontrollably. The expression on his round, baby face was one of pure terror, the absolute vulnerability of the helpless, the suffering of one who had not asked to be born. At that moment a bonding took place between us. I knew I could never leave John alone and defenseless. I realized with my conscious mind what had been up to now the primeval instinct of the lioness protecting her young. This realization dawned in the instant it took me to reach his bed.

"John-John scared, Mamma!" he whimpered.

"Hush, now, darling. Everything is all right. It was just a bad dream. You're safe. Mamma's here. Now go back to sleep," I cooed, hugging him tightly and rocking him back and forth.

Seth was awake now and began to pressure me to come back with him to the Family.

"But I want a different kind of life for the children," I pleaded. "I don't want to drag them around the world, begging for a living. I don't want that anymore, Seth. I've had enough!"

"But, Melita," he argued," you're turning your back on God. You would become a Systemite again—as the Bible says, 'As a dog returneth to his vomit' (Prov. 26:11). Living with the Family is the only true way to serve God. Can't you see that?"

"Not anymore, Seth," I answered. "I've known the hard, cold realities of living on charity. I remember how the leaders turned John and me out on the streets of Stockholm when I was pregnant with Michael, to fend for ourselves while they lived in luxury. The children have suffered enough. What kind of future would they have, begging on the streets all their lives and living in a religious brothel? No, Seth, I'm having no more of it!" I turned off the light to signal an end to our conversation.

"Ah . . . Rich has won you over to the Devil," murmured Seth, as he turned over.

During the next few weeks, relations between Seth and me grew unbearably strained. Whenever we were alone, he moved in to coerce me through fear and guilt to return to the Family. But he showed no guilt at all that his family was living like parasites off the generosity of my parents.

"Those who preach the Gospel should live by the Gospel," Moses David had taught. Though my parents provided for us without complaint, I felt ashamed when I had to ask my mother for money for food, diapers, or laundry. We were parasites. But that was how the Family had taught us to live.

In the evenings, we filled out the reams of required forms for my U.S. visa application. One evening my mother, unable to restrain herself, confronted Seth with some of the doctrines he had been preaching ever since our arrival.

"Seth, you speak about how the Family lives and works to show God's love to people. But Una tells me that your leader teaches having sex relations to demonstrate God's love. Do you mean that you would want Una, your wife and the mother of your children, to go to bed with another man to show 'God's love?' "

"Yes, Mrs. McManus," Seth answered firmly. "I would share my wife to win a soul."

My mother turned pale. Progressive shades of horror passed panoramically across her face. Now she had heard the awful truth for herself.

"Seth, don't . . . don't you see how horribly wrong that is?"

"Oh, Mrs. McManus," Seth chuckled condescendingly. "You see, God's only law is love, and to show God's love through sex is not a sin. Sex is a human need and meeting needs with God's love is good. It is God's will for us to win the world through Christ's love."

I glanced at my mother. She looked stunned. The conversation lapsed into an awkward, brittle silence. Seth, oblivious to the impact of his words said lightheartedly, "Well, I think I'll go to bed now. A good night to all."

I breathed a sigh of relief as he closed the door behind him. The only peace I had was when I was away from him. I turned to my distraught mother.

"Oh, Una, I can't believe it! I can't believe that any decent man would use his wife like that! Why, it's prostitution, plain and simple, no matter how he tries to parade it as God's love. Una, dear, why didn't you tell us about this earlier? We would have come for you and the children!"

"But, Mammy, I was afraid to leave. We were taught that God would be angry and punish us, maybe even kill us, if we left. As for the prostitution, that was the last straw. I could never submit my children to that kind of life—even if it does mean I am damned." Subconsciously, I was still judging my behavior by Mo's standards.

"Una," she said, close to tears, "this is all our fault. I feel so guilty for letting you go when you were too young to know your own mind. But you were so headstrong and we were afraid of losing you forever. They seemed like such a nice, clean-cut group of do-gooders. If we had only known how corrupt and filthy they really were . . ." She shook her head sadly, suddenly looking very old and tired.

The weeks with Seth dragged painfully by. His constant preaching was tearing me apart. Though I was convinced that Moses and the Children of God were terribly wrong, perhaps even dangerous, I had not learned how to defend my new convictions. And Seth's constant verbal harassment was delaying my adjustment to normal living.

I knew I had to get away from him—at least for a while.

My chance came unexpectedly.

Seth had decided to accompany me and the children

to the States for a visit with his mother in Akron, Ohio. Perhaps he felt that with a bit more time, he could persuade me to return to the cult. But a problem with my visa brought a change of plans. There would be a delay of several months before my visa was cleared. In the meantime the children could enter the States on Seth's American passport.

As a guilt-ridden cult casualty, I desperately needed to be free of responsibility—to have some time away from my husband's incessant harping, and even from the normal demands made by my beloved children. Time for my wounds to heal; time to recover my identity.

"Seth, why don't you go ahead and take the boys to your Mom's house?" I suggested. "When my visa comes through, I'll join you. Once we're together again, we can work out our differences and decide what to do about the children."

My parents were as relieved as I when he agreed to the arrangement.

My father and I drove my little family to the airport. I kissed my curly blonde toddler and chubby infant as they smiled unknowingly in their double stroller. While the stewardess checked the tickets, my father tactfully slipped away to the gift shop where he browsed among the books.

"Well, I guess this is it," Seth grinned down at me.

"Yeah, I guess it's my turn to say 'See you in America,' " I replied.

He bent down and kissed me on the cheek. I stood watching as Seth and the stroller with my babies disappeared behind the orange partition. I felt no searing sorrow at the parting. That would come later. Right now, I could feel only a great burden lifting.

18
Deprogramming Myself

"I'm tired, I think I'll turn in," I yawned and stretched as the TV movie came to an end. I looked over at my mother who was dozing peacefully in her chair. I tucked the comforter around her and turned to climb the stairs to my room.

Suddenly, standing at the bottom of the stairs, I was paralyzed with fear. I felt like a small child again. The terrifying darkness was filled with apparitions and unseen horrors.

Get a grip on yourself. This is ridiculous, I thought.

I forced myself to climb the first four steps. I could hear my heart pounding loudly. I stood still, straining to hear any telltale noises from upstairs. All I could hear was the eerie sound of the wind moaning through the weeping willow at the lower end of the garden.

I turned and ran back to the safety of the lighted living room. I turned on another program and waited until my parents were ready for bed before braving the upstairs again.

Night after night the pattern repeated itself. I sat up late talking with mother or watching third-rate TV movies to avoid going upstairs alone. Even when my parents went up to bed and I followed them to my own room, my sleep was haunted by nightmares.

The dreams were always the same. I was running down an endless maze of cobbled streets, each street leading into another one just like the last. Ancient European buildings towering overhead leered at me through their empty windows. The sun beat down on the cobbled stones while I ran as fast as I could, pushing my weary body on by force of will.

Behind me I could hear "them" coming. "They" were angry. "They" wanted to hurt me. Frantically, I pounded on doors and called for help. But no one answered. The houses were deserted. The sun continued to beat down, sapping my strength. I could hear the terrifying sound of angry voices. Finally, I found an open door and quickly slipped inside. In a little room on the third floor, I crouched behind a large, wooden chest in front of a window. I was safe. They would never find me here. I waited and held my breath in fear that the sound of my breathing might betray my hiding place. But I could hear them moving around downstairs. Then the sound of heavy boots on the stairs. I jumped up screaming in horror as the Children of God burst in the door! I screamed louder and louder and threw myself out the window. I heard the shattering of glass and felt the timeless sensation of falling. From the open window drifted the sound of laughter . . .

I woke up, my palms cold and sweaty. With a start, I realized I was clutching the sides of the bed to save myself from falling . . .

It was well over a year before these dreams left me.

I had never heard the word *deprogramming* before Moses David described it in a letter. In the letter he viciously attacked a man named Ted Patrick, claiming Patrick was an instrument of the Devil who kidnapped disciples and brainwashed them. If Patrick ever got his hands on us, Mo insisted, he would stop at nothing— beatings, mental torture, rape—to force us to give up our faith, to "deprogram" us from the "truth."

Unwittingly, as soon as I was free from Seth's daily

sermons, I began to deprogram *myself*. I decided I had heard enough of the Children of God's claims and was determined to examine the other side of the story.

I haunted the libraries and Christian bookstores for material to educate myself on the subject of cults. I found a tract entitled "Beware—'The Children of God'" written by a one-time sponsor. My former leaders had held up this tract to ridicule, but now I read it slowly and thoughtfully. Several points in the pamphlet struck a responsive chord.

> You may say that this movement has helped you in many ways, which may be true. Many so-called 'Christian' cults also contain a lot of good, but a glass of pure water can become fatal by one drop of poison! It is not enough to claim that because 'Moses' started this outreach he must be right, for history is full of good men who subsequently fell. Remember that Satan himself was Lucifer meaning Light bearer; he proudly exalted himself against God and fell . . .
>
> The Children of God can well boast of many converts who know now the love of Jesus, but they are told that this justifies the whole movement. Whereas at this point their greatest responsibility begins—to feed those babes in Christ on the pure Word of God. Even this they claim to do, but with this food the poison of Mo's letters must be added . . .
>
> Jesus had this kind of deception in mind when he said—'Beware of false prophets, which come to you in sheep's clothing, but inwardly they are ravening wolves. By their fruits ye shall know them" (Matthew 7:15–16). The 'bad fruits' of the movement are not evident on the surface, but are painfully so in their

Letters and practices, including—

Bitter abuse and defamation of parents, Christians and any who cross their path.

Rejection of God-ordained authority, or 'system.'

Hypocrisy and double standards in public relations; Evasion of truth, and secrecy.

Immoral insinuations against our Lord.

Laxity in morals, language, etc.

Strict obedience to leadership—even if they are wrong.

Married couples and families separated.

Perversion of scriptures to justify these errors.

Exaltation of 'Moses' letters' to the level of scripture.

I thought carefully about each of these teachings that the Christian writer had categorized as 'bad fruit'— indicative of a false prophet. Thinking clearly, without Seth or any of the leaders to influence me, I could not rationalize or deny these perversions of scripture and Christian doctrine. I could no longer believe their notions that "freedom is slavery" and "love is hate."

As the peaceful days crept by, my fogged perceptions began to clear. I looked critically at the doctrines of the Children of God and discovered that "I," the original person, did not really believe them.

Encouraged by this new clarity of thought, I sat down and wrote a long, apologetic letter to Rich. I explained to him how I had been duped into sleeping with him by the Mo letters. Then I breathed a sigh of relief as I put the letter in the mailbox. I was making progress in putting back together the pieces of my shattered life.

I read *All God's Children* by Stoner and Parke and *Let Our Children Go* by Ted Patrick. I began to see a pattern of conversion and beliefs that cult members hold in common, no matter what name the cult bears. We were all recruited with a bombardment of "love" and pressured into giving up thinking for ourselves. We were expected to follow our leaders blindly. We all went through different degrees of alienation from our families and isolation from the world. Each cult proclaimed itself to be the bearer of the "truth." Fear of God's punishment for defection was instilled in all of us. Our lives were controlled and directed by someone who claimed to be God or, at the very least, God's most recent and greatest prophet. We lived in poverty while our leaders lived well, some even in luxury. We were taught to actively repress any critical analysis or complaints about the group as "thoughts of the Devil." We were all reduced to the level of helpless children, dependent on our leaders as parents and rulers. We were systematically worn down by a routine of insufficient rest and food; constant indoctrination; feelings of fear and guilt; disorientation and isolation; by physical and verbal humiliation and a prohibition of thinking or reading what we wanted. We were, in short, fanatics.

As I avidly read Ted Patrick's account of bringing people back to reality through the deprogramming process, I came across the name of a young woman from Ohio. Little did I know that within a year I would meet this woman, Marcia Carroll, and she would become one of my dearest and closest friends. Her love and faith in me would make a huge contribution to my emotional and psychological recovery. And through her, I would become part of a genuinely Christian congregation.

Meanwhile, I began to prowl around the employment offices and found a temporary job as a waitress. Work had an energizing effect on me, and I felt my old zest returning. Meeting the daily challenge of doing my job well, I felt worthwhile again—human, normal, and productive. On Fridays, my pay envelope enhanced my feeling of self-respect.

"I can see this job is good for you, Una, dear," my mother said. "The old glow and rosiness is back in your cheeks. Your daddy can't get over the change in you. He feels he has rediscovered you after all those years of sullen silence. After all this time, you are our friend."

My dad and I spent hours listening to music and talking and laughing as we hadn't done since I was a child.

"You know, Chick," he said one day, "I've always thought you had the ability to be a writer. You should start making notes and write a book describing your experiences."

I pounced on the idea and began to read widely. Words became my friends. I read Dostoevsky, Gibran, Solzhenitsyn, and Joyce. I submerged myself in great literature. I wallowed in books that had been denied me in the cult.

With the fascination of a child, I felt my mind unfolding like a flower. I found myself constantly celebrating my freedom, telling myself "I can think! I can learn! Nobody is telling me what to think and what not to think anymore."

"Una, you're such a changed person since you left that horrible group," my mother cried one day in delight. "Your whole appearance has changed. You look well and happy now. Promise me you'll never go back to that gang of crazies."

"You don't have to worry about that," I said, laughing at such an absurd notion. "I would never allow myself to be conned into anything like that again. I'm back to stay!"

We hugged each other. The fact that there was true love outside the cult was dawning slowly on me. I began to see the "love" inside the Children of God for what it really was—a sales technique used for recruiting new members. Their love was a charade masking dominance, cruelty, subservience, and immorality. Now I no longer had to think of my parents as Satan's cohorts bent on corrupting me. Now I could appreciate, enjoy, and love them for the good friends they had become.

19
In Mysterious Ways

Invading all the golden moments and vying with the joy of rediscovery was a deep sadness.

As I walked home from work each day, I watched the young mothers parading their babies in their prams. Often, I took the long way so I could stop by a certain toy shop displaying a white teddy bear, much like one we had bought for Michael. The little bear became a tangible link with my missing children. With a lump in my throat, I would hurry home to check the day's mail. It seemed as though my visa would never come.

The children appeared more and more often in my dreams—dreams so poignant and so real that I would reach for the boys, waking to find myself grasping only air.

But the months slipped by and still no visa. The leaves of the forest turned to russet and gold as time marched on towards winter. And the wind grew as cold and bitter as Seth's letters.

"Coming here [to America] has only strengthened my convictions that we [the cult] have the one and only answer to this whole mess," he wrote. "What America needs is not a revival, but a total, absolute Revolution— if necessary, a spiritually *violent* Revolution for Jesus."

"I won't be here much longer . . . I'm sorry, but I'm finished with you . . . Your kind of treachery is not my cup of tea."

"Don't blame the Family if you are mixed up! You have only yourself to blame!"

With new-found fortitude, I responded.

"No, Seth, I'm not going to blame myself anymore for the sins of Moses David. I have no more reverence for my torturer, no more desire to absorb my enemy's guilt."

And finally: "Seth, I get the impression that you want to end our relationship. Am I right?"

I couldn't get a straight answer to that question. In one letter or phone call his tone was gentle and tender; in the next, he was furious and threatened divorce. But a constant theme that ran through all his communication was his plan to take the children to a colony as soon as I arrived in the United States. I was frantic!

"I wonder if I'll ever see them again, Mammy!" I sobbed. "Everything seems so hopeless. How can I fight Seth? He is determined to keep the children in the cult. And I know no one in America to help me. What am I to do?"

"Don't worry, dear," she said comfortingly, "you'll be back with them in God's good time."

God. That alienated Friend. It had been a very long time since I had spoken to Him. I couldn't believe He could let me be so deceived in His name. I decided that if He were there at all, He would have to understand I couldn't cope with religion just now. He'd have to excuse my ignoring Him and be there when I needed Him. I could no longer force myself to believe what someone else had said I *should* believe. I would not use religion as a crutch. God would just have to understand.

I discussed these thoughts with Father Murphy, the small, round-faced priest in our parish.

"I think you're right, Una," he said agreeably, his dark eyes twinkling. "You've had a traumatic blow to your faith. It will take time to heal, but God will be there when you need Him. He'll wait—He's not going anywhere!

"I think your attitude and unwillingness to use religion as a crutch is a sign of thoughtful maturity. I'm not worried about you, Una. You'll make it. I have faith in your intelligence—and in God too. In time you will discover Him again."

Father Murphy's words were reassuring, but as one bleak day followed another, I began to lose hope. It seemed I had saved myself, but lost my children. And God, once more, seemed very far away.

There seemed to be no alternative. I called Seth and said with resignation, "You win. I can't stop you from taking the children. But *please* tell me where you will be. Maybe I could get a job in the same city so I could be near the boys."

"Yeah, maybe," he replied coolly. "I can't guarantee how long we would be in any one city. We have to keep mobile to spread the Gospel into all the world before Jesus comes. You might have a hard time following us. In fact, you'd better think seriously about coming over here at all."

"There's not much hope then?" I asked tearfully.

"No," he snapped. In the background I could hear Michael crying.

"Mike is just waking up from his nap," Seth said hurriedly. "I've got to go."

Then he was gone. A wave of helplessness engulfed me. My child was crying on the other side of the world and there was nothing I could do to help him. I sat listening to the dead sound of the line while my tears trickled down into the mouthpiece. In time, I replaced the receiver and crept up to bed.

That night I dreamed I was with the children on an outing. We were chattering and laughing gaily. I woke up, still talking to John, to be answered by the silence of my empty room.

Sometimes, into the blackest night sky, a shimmering star will suddenly come into view. We may perceive it as having appeared from nowhere, when in reality, the star was always there.

Hope at last appeared for me in the person of Judge Wallace. Having learned of my situation from my parents, he arranged a meeting. As I knocked on his door, I prayed earnestly that he would be able to help me.

"Well, well, so you're Una," Judge Wallace boomed in his gruff, kindly voice. "Come into the study, my dear. We've a lot to talk about."

I settled down in a comfortable chair by the fireplace and glanced around the cozy room. It was interestingly irregular, its nooks and crannies filled with little tables and shelves displaying various knick-knacks. The handsome bookshelves by the fireplace contained books dealing with the law and with Christianity.

The big man leaned forward, his bushy eyebrows knit with concern.

"Well, Una, I understand you've been through a hard time. Tell me your story and I will see what assistance I can be to you."

The words came tumbling out—the corruption of the Family; my decision to leave; most of all, my present dilemma over my children.

"And Seth says he is going to take them to a Children of God colony, where I may never see them again. I have no way to stop him."

The Judge looked grave and furrowed his brow. Finally, he spoke:

"There really isn't anything you can do from here. For you to regain custody of the children through the English courts, Seth would have to be on English soil."

As he paused, my countenance fell. "Now don't lose heart. There is something we can do. You see, I am a member of the 'Lawyers' Christian Fellowship.' This is an organization of lawyers, dedicated to the 'Great Commission'; it was founded here in London in the last century. In 1957 it was taken to America by a fine Christian woman, Leda Hartwell. Mrs. Hartwell now lives in Columbus, Ohio. She might be able to help you . . ."

Just then the telephone rang. "It's for you, Jack," the judge's wife called. "Hurry, dear. It's long distance."

I paced the room, waiting for Judge Wallace to return. I gazed out at the meticulously manicured garden. *Maybe it's hopeless*, I thought dismally. *Maybe I'm just on a wild goose chase. If Seth is not on English soil, there is nothing anyone can do . . .*

"Well, well, what a remarkable coincidence," the judge mused as he hurried into the room. "Or more likely—Providence! That call was from none other than Leda Hartwell, the lady lawyer I just mentioned!"

He settled into his chair, his eyes twinkling with excitement.

"The dear lady has never called me before. Today she calls on business concerning the Fellowship. When I told her your story, she said she would be delighted to take your case. What's more, her office is located very near the home of your mother-in-law, where you'll be staying! I'll give you Mrs. Hartwell's address and the two of you can take it from there. Yes, my dear, the Lord is at work here. I'm sure of it!"

I skipped merrily home, clutching the precious address. "This is it! This is it!" I thought ecstatically. "The break I've been waiting for." I even dared to think, as Judge Wallace had suggested, that God might be working for me behind the scenes.

Now the wheels were irrevocably set in motion. I had the legal leverage I needed. My visa had finally come. As promised, my brother-in-law Rich would sponsor me as a legal alien in the United States.

I left before dawn on a murky September morning.

As my father backed the car out of the garage, I stood beside my mother in the open doorway. She was shivering in her dressing gown. Mingled with the joyful anticipation of being reunited with my children was a poignant sadness. I was leaving my parents just as I was beginning to know and enjoy them. My mother shivered again and drew her wrap tighter. Though she said goodbye in a voice that didn't quaver, her eyes seemed to focus on some distant object as is her habit when she is hurt or unhappy.

"Bye, Mammy." I hugged her and fought back my own tears. "Don't worry, I'll see you again. I promise."

20
Kidnapped!

"Ladies and gentlemen, we are now approaching New York City," the pilot announced. The long flight from London was almost over.

I looked out at the grey land mass below. America! John and Michael's new home—and mine. Throughout the entire trip I had thought of them, planning what I would say to them, imagining what it would be like seeing them after six months. I would arrive late at night, slip into their room, and watch them sleep before waking them to see the surprise and joy on their sleepy faces. Or perhaps Seth would keep them up to greet me. I counted the hours until I would be with them again.

In Kennedy Airport I stood in line, waiting my turn to be admitted into the land of hope and opportunity. The line inched forward with agonizing slowness. I thought about my Irish ancestors—immigrants, like myself, who had come to this great land of promise searching for their dream. I felt a strong bond with them.

The weary man in the glass case stamped my papers and waved me through. I crossed the magical line. I was in America!

My first step was to phone Seth's mother in Akron. As I waited for the phone to ring, I absorbed my first impressions of America. I was awed by the number of big cars jamming the streets and relieved to find that

Americans are not a race of tourists armed with cameras and binoculars.

"He's gone, Una," my mother-in-law answered in a choked voice.

"Gone? Seth's gone?" I echoed.

"He left yesterday. He's taken the kids to a colony in Columbus."

I felt shocked and dazed. My eagerness to reach Akron approached panic. I fretted for the rest of the journey, remembering that Moses encouraged his disciples to flee the country with their children if their mate left the group. If I didn't catch up with Seth soon, the chances were good that I would never see my children again.

Shortly before midnight I arrived at the small white house where Seth and the children had been living. An attractive lady met me at the door.

"Welcome, Una. I'm Gail," she said, extending her hand.

I relaxed. She was warm and friendly and I liked her right away.

"I'm sorry Greg and the children aren't here."

"Greg? Is Seth going by his legal name now?"

"Oh, yes, we don't call him by his cult name anymore. He's gone. But there's nothing we can do about it tonight and you must be exhausted from your trip."

Gail showed me to a cheerful, inviting bedroom. Greg and the boys had slept here in the last twenty-four hours. I paced around the room, sifting for clues. All I found was one child's dirty sock and a paint-splashed, tattered T-shirt belonging to John. I went to sleep holding them and praying that I would find the children before they disappeared forever.

I slept fitfully and awoke early, impatient to begin our search. Gail's report on the children's welfare was encouraging. At least, Greg had been a good father—teaching them to read and count and telling them Bible stories. I couldn't help wondering if he had been following the child care letters in the area of discipline, too.

When I phoned Mrs. Hartwell, she was just as eager as I to start work on the case, and offered to drive me to Columbus. There, we would follow the few leads we had.

On the trip, I found this small, vibrant woman in her early sixties to be lively company. She listened with keen interest as I unfolded the latest developments in my story, occasionally probing gently for more detail.

"You see, Mrs. Hartwell," I concluded, "until Judge Wallace put me in touch with you, I had no hope of getting the children back. Now it seems Greg has made good on his threat to take them to a colony as soon as I came to America. But my main worry is that he will leave the state or even the country . . ."

"I've done my homework, Una," she nodded. You have a legitimate concern. But there are several Children of God colonies in this area and I don't intend to rest until we find your boys and expose this whole corrupt organization for what it is!"

We located the colony house with little trouble. Standing outside the door, I paused to draw a deep breath. I had traveled halfway around the world for this moment. Then I walked through the open doorway— and into Greg's path.

"What on earth are you doing here?" he said gruffly. His face registered no delight at seeing me, no joy— only surprise and disgust. I felt like a worm that had crawled in from the garden.

"Well, here I am, all the way from England," I stammered, trying to hide my disappointment and hurt. Seth/Greg had put on some weight and his hair had grown. He looked good, more like the man I had married. Our eyes locked for a long moment. I searched for some flicker of warmth and affection, but found none.

He stood there, cold and distant, making no move to greet me beyond his initial curt remark. Hurt and confused, I looked away.

In an adjoining room, some children were playing— pretty little girls in bouncy dresses and neat little boys. One little girl was reading a Moses David letter designed for children. They seemed to be carefree and content, except for one forlorn little toddler. His hair was unkempt, and he walked slowly and sadly, dragging a battered toy behind him. He looked up at me with great mournful eyes, then continued on his solitary way.

"And who is that child?" I asked, moved by his wistful expression.

"Why, that's Michael. He's walking now. The summer sun turned his hair blonde."

A lump rose in my throat as I looked down on my little son whom I hadn't recognized. I knelt down and held out my arms to him.

"Come to Mamma, Michael," I coaxed.

He looked at me with distrust and ran crying to Greg.

As Greg comforted Michael, a small curly-haired figure appeared in the doorway.

"Mom!" John screeched in a newly-acquired American accent. He threw himself into my arms and launched into a detailed description of the day's events as if we had never been parted.

I put my face in my hands and began to sob loudly. Greg put his arms around my shoulders in a condescending manner, as if I were a vile sinner suffering justly, and prayed aloud for Jesus to help me.

I drew away from his pious, self-righteous embrace and faced him squarely.

"Now that I'm here, I want to know exactly what you intend to do with my children."

"Why, we are going to stay here with the Family and serve the Lord," he chuckled. "What else did you expect me to do? You can come and visit the children while we're in Columbus—as long as you don't interrupt the colony activities."

I bristled with indignation. For the first time in my life, I stood up to him.

"You're not taking my children away from me," I said boldly. "You're not going to separate me from them again. They are my children, too, and I'm not letting you drag them into this web of perversion. I'm not budging from this house and neither you nor your puny leaders can make me do otherwise."

Greg was startled by this display of open defiance.

"Is that so?" he mumbled. "Well, well, we'll see about that." Quickly he disappeared up a rickety staircase.

I sat down in a stuffed chair and called John over. His blue eyes widened with delight as I unfolded the treasures I had brought him from England. While he lay on the floor playing with his new bus, I tried to persuade Michael to sit on my lap. He refused to come near me and slunk into a far corner with his toy.

"But, Michael, this is your Mamma . . . don't you remember?" John cried. But Michael didn't remember and wouldn't be persuaded.

Half an hour later Greg returned—no longer troubled or confused. His features had settled into the plastic complacency of one who follows orders, one who has shifted the responsibility for making decisions to others.

A couple, whom I guessed to be the colony leaders, accompanied him. The man, in his late twenties, was fat and flabby. The woman, standing behind him, affected a sickly, sweet demeanor.

"I've counseled with my leaders and we have prayed about this situation . . ." Greg began, baring his even teeth in a forced smile. "Mark, our shepherd, thinks I should take you and the children back to my mother's house in Akron until we sort our problems out. Your

presence here would just be a bad influence on the rest
of the colony."

John sat beside me on the bus, chattering incessantly,
while Michael sat beside John, serious and quiet. He did
not smile until he ran to meet Gail's big dog. I was
relieved to see he could still express happiness, but I
was concerned about the change that had taken place in
him during our six-month separation. He had changed
from a bouncing, laughing baby into a somber, silent,
toddler. Was he wrenched away from me too quickly
and too soon? Hadn't Greg shown him enough affection? Had Greg been too harsh in his discipline? I would
never know what had transpired during my absence, but
I was determined to see Michael a happy child once
more.

As I cuddled the boys in Gail's living room, Greg
eyed the scene disapprovingly.

"Put the children down. That's enough molly-
coddling," he barked.

Fighting the old impulse to submit mindlessly, I answered firmly, "No, Greg. I haven't seen the children in
six months. Now more than ever I need to show them
affection."

He snorted in disgust and went into the kitchen,
grumbling under his breath that a "backslider" was not
capable of real love.

His attacks continued into the night. "You're a child
of Satan. You have chosen the world. Now you'll have
to pay for it."

During the day we couldn't carry on a conversation
without quarrelling bitterly. He used Scriptures to condemn my unbelief of the cult and I reviled him for his
slavish adherence to the teachings of a perverted old
man.

For the first time Gail heard about the new com-
mandments practiced by the cult: begging in the streets,

the mandatory religious prostitution, the advocation of child sex. She was horror-stricken.

After four bitter days of tension, Greg decided to return to the mindless haven of the Family. Gail threatened to get custody of the children if he dared take them with him. Greg was furious.

When he was ready to leave, he knelt beside John, took his hands and, looking straight into his eyes, said gravely, "John-John, I want you to understand what's happening. I have to leave because your Mamma doesn't love God and Jesus anymore. She doesn't want to serve God anymore. Daddy wants to serve God and that's why he has to leave. Your Grandma and your Mamma have got it set up so that if I take you and Michael with me, the police will come and take you away from me. So I have to leave you both here. I'll pray for you. I'm sorry." He kissed John and left quickly with tears on his cheeks.

The weeks slipped by pleasantly. Indian summer came, warming the air. Michael, too, began to warm up to me and smiled more often. I spent my days caring for the children—feeding and washing them, teaching them, and taking them to the school playground down the street. At Gail's suggestion, when my money ran out, I reported to the Welfare Office and explained that my husband had deserted me and my two young children to join a religious cult. We began to receive welfare benefits and I made plans to enter journalism school as soon as the children were old enough to go to a day care center.

Then one evening Greg called. Gail spoke to him first. I sat at the kitchen table watching her face light up.

"You're coming back? That's wonderful!" she exclaimed, smiling at me. My initial reaction was suspicion. This was probably another cheap trick. The Children of God would stop at nothing to get what they wanted, and they wanted my children.

Skeptically, I listened to Greg's plea.

"I love you, Una, and I love our children . . . That's why I want to come back. I can't live without you. I'm having real doubts about the Family and this Flirty Fishing business . . . Please take me back. I really do love you, you know . . ."

I was still suspicious when he walked through the door that night. But as the days passed and he continued to be a loving and considerate husband and father, my doubts melted away and I began to hope for our future.

"I love you and the kids so much that I had to come back. I couldn't leave you, not even for Moses David," he whispered in my ear as we lay warm and comfortable together in the still, quiet darkness.

"Where did you go after you left here?" I asked, snuggling against his bare chest.

"I was sent on the road alone to Toledo. Litnessing went really badly there and I was lonely. I had a lot of time to think about you and the kids. I decided it wasn't worth it to give you up. So I left the Family and now I'm back where I belong."

My heart ached for him as I recalled the feelings of despair and failure when the Mo letters weren't selling well.

"It's all over now," I soothed, brushing the hair from his forehead. "You're home and we can start a new life together. Let's put the whole awful experience of the Children of God behind us."

"A new life," he sighed. "Hey, I've been thinking. I can use my veteran's benefits to go back to school and get a teaching certificate. And it's about time we had our own place, don't you think?"

"Our own home!" I exclaimed in delight. "Where we could be a real family? That would be fantastic!"

Greg spent the next few days arranging the details of

his G.I. Bill grant for school and his veteran's housing loan. He visited several schools to inspect their programs. I was euphoric as we planned our future.

On Greg's sixth day home, I left the children with him while I kept a doctor's appointment.

The setting sun was splashing the late afternoon sky with delicate hues of orange and gold. On the walk home I had time to absorb its splendor and revel in my new happiness. When I reached Gail's house, I found Greg's younger brother George sitting on the couch reading. The house was quiet.

"Hi, Una. Greg took the kids down to the library. They should be back any minute."

"Good idea. They have an excellent children's section," I said as I headed for the kitchen. "Would you like to stay for dinner, George? We're having spaghetti—Irish style!"

"Sounds great. Thanks a lot."

At 6:30, George commented that Greg was late.

"Yes, he is," I said absently as I stirred the sauce. "Oh, he probably just lost track of the time, or maybe he stopped at the store for something. We don't have to wait if you're hungry."

By 7:30 Greg had still not come home. I tried to ignore the sinking feeling in my stomach. I turned off the stove and began to put away the food. George sat silently in front of his plate, drumming his fingers on the table. At eight o'clock he stood up.

"Listen, Una, I hate leaving you alone when you are worried like this, but I've got to go. Greg is just late. There is some excuse, I know. Don't worry, okay? Mom should be home from work before too long. You have my number if you need me."

Then George was gone. I sat down and tried to read, tried to believe that Greg wouldn't do such a thing to me. I told myself over and over that he would be home in a few minutes. The wind howled around the house, making soft, moaning sounds—like the cries of small children.

I watched the hands of the clock creep around to eight-thirty. The library must be closing by now. I dialed the library's number. No man with two boys in a double stroller had been there that day. It was true . . .

Shaking now, I telephoned George.

"George," I whispered hoarsely, "Greg has kidnapped the kids. He didn't go to the library today. He has taken them back to the cult . . . His coming home was all a trick—a lie. Everything he said about leaving the Family because he loved me was all a dirty, rotten lie."

21
The
Seige

I sat on the couch, stunned. My mind whirled in confusion as policemen moved in and out of the house, asking questions and collecting data for the missing persons report.

"I'll help you find them, Una," said George quietly. "Even though Greg is my brother, what he has done is wrong."

We decided to look in the most obvious place first. We arrived at the Columbus colony shortly before ten o'clock that night. A brother finally answered our persistent knocking and admitted us into the living room.

"I demand to know if Seth and my children are here." My voice was shaking with emotion.

"Yes, Seth is here with his children," smiled the young man, apparently unaware of who I was.

"So you followed me."

I swung around and found myself facing Greg. He stood squarely with his arms folded defiantly across his chest.

"Ha! I see George brought you. Betrayed by my wife and now my brother!"

"You lied to me and deceived me," I said coldly. "I suppose by your code that is justifiable in the name of God's love."

"Sure, I deceived you. I was planning to take the kids

all along. You see, I can't trust you. You are on the side of the Devil now and I can't expose my children to your Satanic influence.

"I have the children, and I'm going to keep them," he taunted. "Possession is nine-tenths of the law, you know. You'll have to leave now. You've caused enough disturbance."

"I'm not leaving until I see my children," I said. "You can't keep my own children from me."

Greg looked to Mark, the colony shepherd, for an answer.

"I'm renting this house," Mark said to me, "so you have no legal rights to stay. I'm telling you—get out of here."

"Ho, ho! So now you show your true colors!" I laughed scornfully. "So this is the 'love of God' you preach—love that won't allow a mother to see her own children. Order me off your property all you want, but *I'm not leaving until I see my children.*"

Greg looked imploringly at Mark.

"Well, I suppose she could see them for a minute," Mark granted grandly, "but she is not to go upstairs. Bring the children down here."

Greg brought John and Michael down the steps, sound asleep in their pajamas, one on each shoulder.

"Here they are," he turned around so I could catch a glimpse of their faces, then hurried away before I could reach them.

I had to get out before I broke down completely. Grabbing George's arm, I lunged for the door.

"You're not going to get away with this," I shouted after Greg.

My fingers were stiff with the cold as I telephoned my lawyer from a nearby gas station.

"He's done it now, Mrs. Hartwell," I said. "Greg has kidnapped the children and is holding them at the colony on Summit Street. They would only let me see the children for a minute or two. The leader ordered me off the property. I . . . I'm very much afraid that Greg will take the children out of the country and I'll never see them again . . . You've got to do something, Mrs. Hartwell," I cried desperately.

"Well, dear, to be honest, this couldn't have come at a worse time. It's Friday night and the courts are closed until Monday. But I'll telephone a judge and see what can be done. In the meantime, you and your brother-in-law watch the house very carefully. He mustn't leave under any circumstances."

The first long, cold night of the three-day siege had begun. George and I stayed up all night watching the front and back doors of the house. Toward morning my feet were so cold I could barely feel them.

The weekend stretched into an interminable night-mare relieved only by quick snacks and hot coffee. We dared not close our eyes for a second. We sat on the ground outside the colony telling passersby that my children were being held inside the house, kidnapped by a religious cult. Some stopped and sympathized. Others hurried by, afraid of becoming involved.

Walking up and down the sidewalk like a pacing lio-ness, I called out, "John! Michael!" and felt my heart break when I heard them answer, "Mommy!" and saw their little faces pressed against the window. I ran to beat on the door, but as soon as Mark recognized me, he slammed the door in my face.

"Maybe *I* can talk some sense into him," said George at last. "Maybe he'll listen to me since I'm his brother."

But he, too, was unsuccessful. "It's no use," he signed. "He doesn't even seem like the same guy I grew up with. I couldn't reason with him. If you fell down with exhaustion on their front lawn, they would probably look out the window laughing and say, 'Look what hap-pened to the Devil! Praise the Lord!'"

By midnight of the third day we were exhausted. Despite the freezing walks around the house and the bone-chilling night air pouring in through the open car door windows, both George and I fell asleep. At three o'clock I awoke with a start. The Family's car was gone—dark, empty shadows marking the parking spot. Panicking, I shook George, screaming that Greg must have gotten away.

I ran after a policeman walking his beat. Gasping for breath, I explained what had happened and begged him to accompany me to the Family's house. A little reluctant and dumbfounded by my urgency, the policeman stood stoically beside me as I knocked on the door.

Puffy-faced Mark answered.

"I want to speak to my husband, Greg Philips," I demanded.

"Well, Una," Mark said in a syrupy sweet tone of voice, "I'm afraid Greg has left of his own free will and there is nothing you can do about it. And right now I am asking you to get off my property and there is nothing you can do about that either," he said curtly and slammed the door.

I looked at the policeman in bewilderment.

"I'm afraid he's right, Miss," the officer told me. "We'd better leave. You'll just have to wait until tomorrow and see your lawyer."

I walked slowly back to the car.

"There's nothing we can do, George. He's outwitted us." Blood rushed to my ears. I stared out the window, my eyes blurred by tears. My stomach turned over. "And who knows where he's gone? Maybe he's on his way out of the state right now. Maybe it'll be too late to stop him tomorrow."

"Listen, Una, don't cry. And don't worry. Our lawyer will get 'em."

We kept our lonely vigil until Monday morning.

"Everything's under control," said Mrs. Hartwell

briskly on the telephone. "I've filed for a protective custody order and alimony. That order will stop Greg from taking off with the children. That is—if we can find him and serve him."

"I'm sure the leadership knows where he is," I said hopefully.

"No doubt they do," Mrs. Hartwell replied. "Now you just stay outside that house and wait for the sheriff. When he arrives, go with him to the door. You never know; Greg could be hiding inside. Moving the car could have been another trick. You know, that so-called religious group's tactics are atrocious. If you decide to sue, I'll bet you'd win on grounds of misrepresentation of ideals. They should be stopped before anyone else is hurt."

"Oh! Could we sue them?"

"We certainly can. They can't be allowed to get away with this. You stick with it, girl. We'll get those children, just you wait and see."

I drew strength from Mrs. Hartwell's confidence as I paced the sidewalk. The sheriff, a big, blustery man, arrived shortly. He told me not to fret, for he knew how to handle these people.

The sheriff knocked loudly and flashed his credentials. "I've come to serve Greg Philips," he said firmly to Mark.

Mark's reply sounded memorized. "I'm sorry, sir, but Greg Philips has left here of his own free will and taken his children with him. I have no idea where he is."

"Listen, son, you're dealing with the law here. This is no time to play games," the sheriff thundered. "Now tell Greg Philips that I have papers to serve him. He calls you on the telephone, doesn't he?"

Mark mumbled an affirmative reply. His brave, cocksure veneer was cracking. I watched his double chin trembling. The sheriff left with a stern warning.

Outside, he shook my hand and wished me luck. "That's a frightened man," he assured me. "He knows he will be in real trouble if he hides your husband from the law. We'll get your kids."

"We'll get your kids . . . we'll get your kids." I tried to convince myself on the long, silent trip home.

Greg called shortly after we arrived at Gail's. He said he had received word from the sheriff and was ready to release the children to me. He was waiting for us at the Columbus bus station.

Greg rode back to Akron with us, preaching to us all the way. But he didn't stay. He would have no part of the Devil's kingdom. He had to go back and serve the Lord with King David.

22

"Nothing Short of Miraculous"

The courtroom buzzed with activity. I sat nervously beside my attorney, Mr. William Hewitt, Mrs. Hartwell's colleague. Greg and his lawyer took their places. Court reporters hovered like birds of prey, waiting for tidbits that would become tomorrow's news. In the stands sat two women I did not recognize.

"The woman with the reddish hair is Mrs. Marian Carroll," Mr. Hewitt whispered. "She gave me a copy of the report on the Children of God by the Attorney General of New York. Her daughter is a former cult member, so she knows the ropes."

A hush fell over the courtroom as the judge rapped for attention.

"We will now proceed with the hearing on the application by Una Philips to be appointed the legal guardian of John and Michael, the two minor children of Greg and Una Philips," said Judge Nathan Koplin of Summit County Probate Court. "Please proceed with testimony, Mr. Hewitt."

Mr. Hewitt called Greg to the witness stand. Greg looked ill at ease. I felt sorry for him when he couldn't remember his address or how much money he had personally been responsible for bringing into the cult. However, he lost no time in attacking my character.

"My wife had an affair with my brother when he

came to visit us in Norway," he blurted.

"Under what conditions did she carry on this alleged affair?" Mr. Hewitt demanded.

"Well, you see, we witness to lost sheep—non-members—about Jesus—in discotheques, nightclubs, wherever they can be found. If it comes down to it, we are permitted to go all the way to prove God's love and win a soul. My brother was a lost sheep—but I never expected my wife to go to bed with *him!*"

I couldn't tell if his ego was really bruised or if he was just putting on a convincing act. Anyway, the judge ignored the reference to my infidelity and pursued another line of questioning.

"Are you telling this court that in order to convert persons to your movement, members of your group are instructed to engage in intimate relations with these persons?" the judge was frowning.

"Yes, Your Honor."

"When you and your wife joined this cult, were you informed that you would be required to participate in this kind of activity?"

"Not at first. We didn't hear about it until later."

"Have you, yourself, ever committed adultery to win the soul of a non-member?"

There was a long pause.

"Well, it wasn't really adultery," he replied evasively. "We're just willing to do anything it takes to show people how much God loves them. If that means relieving their sexual needs, we do it."

"There has to be a purpose and a need then," the judge observed. "All that is done is done for the purpose of saving a soul and not for the physical pleasure derived. And this is from the Gospel according to Moses David. Is that correct?"

"Correct, Your Honor," Greg affirmed.

"Then, on your own testimony, your wife had your

permission. So you have nothing to complain about."

The hearing dragged on all day. At the end of the grueling session, Mr. Hewitt remarked:

"Your Honor, obviously this cult is nothing but a scheme, under the guise of religion, to promote organized prostitution for the purpose of making money."

In issuing his order, Judge Koplin commended me. "I admire your spunk, young woman. You apparently have higher ideals than your husband and his friends in this cult. My biggest concern right now is for the welfare of these two children and it is in their best interest that I now place them in the permanent custody of their mother."

"Congratulations!" I turned towards the warm voice and recognized the smiling face of the woman pointed out to me by Mr. Hewitt. "I'm Marian Carroll," she said. "I know this hasn't been easy for you. My daughter, Marcia, has been through a similar experience with another cult, the Divine Light Mission. We had her deprogrammed by Ted Patrick."

"Ted Patrick. I recognize that name. And didn't he mention your daughter in his book? I remember reading that book before I came to the States."

"Right. We have had a lot of dealings with ex-cult members, so we know how difficult it must be for you, especially with no family in this country. Count on us to help if you need us."

I looked at this compassionate, maternal woman and felt her genuine concern.

"Thank you, Mrs. Carroll, we could do with some help. This whole thing has been a terrible shock for my mother-in-law, so we're moving out of her house into our own apartment. I'd love for you and your daughter to come and visit me and the children . . . I get very lonely sometimes."

The court battles left me feeling like a deflated bal-
loon. A few days after the children and I moved into our
new apartment, I came down with the flu. For several
days I lay on a tattered couch—one of the two pieces of
furniture I owned, dragging myself up now and then to
feed and diaper the children. Marian Carroll couldn't
have picked a better time to visit.

"Una, you look dreadful!" she exclaimed. "Why
didn't you call us?"

"Well, I don't have a telephone yet," I shrugged,
"and besides, I didn't want to impose . . ."

"Baloney!" she retorted. "We offered to help and we
mean it! Una, this is my daughter, Marcia."

I shook hands with an attractive, poised young
woman, who generated an aura of self-confidence and
warmth. I liked her immediately.

"My mom told me how well you testified in court. It
took courage to take on the cult," she said with admiration in her voice. "We've brought you a few things we
thought you might need."

Before I could protest, they were bringing in blankets,
sheets, curtains, food, clothes, and various kitchen
utensils.

"I don't know how to thank you!" I exclaimed.

"Well, I know," said Mrs. Carroll. "I want you to sit
right down and make a list of anything else you need.
After what you've done, kiddo, you deserve it."

Trust returns slowly and is built by constant loving
deeds. The Carrolls reached out and accepted me and
my children into their family. We were no longer strangers in a strange land. In Marcia I found a faithful best
friend—a confidante who helped me readjust to normal
life.

"Marcia, you have been away from the Divine Light

Mission for over four years. Did you ever have nightmares where members of the cult are chasing you and you can't get away?" I asked as we sat by the sandbox watching the children play.

"Yes," she said, "but they faded in time. Bad dreams are a pretty common reaction among ex-cult members. Remember, you just can't walk away from a cult. It takes a period of time to recover."

"And what about those who claim that only gullible or immoral people join cults? Don't you feel ashamed or embarrassed when people find out you have been in one?" I asked.

"Listen, Una, most people just don't realize the brainwashing and mind control that goes on in the cults, so don't let their ignorant remarks hurt you. You can try to explain what it was like, but don't expect them to understand completely. And don't let their questions cause you to doubt yourself. Just about anybody could be brainwashed into a cult, so it wasn't because you were gullible or stupid or immoral. It was simply a matter of being in the wrong place at the wrong time," Marcia answered confidently.

"But I'm plagued by feelings of worthlessness," I confided. "I feel that I'm just no good. I've messed up my life once. Maybe I'll do it again."

"Una, you've got to give yourself more credit for what you have accomplished since you left the cult," she said emphatically. "Coming to a strange country; fighting for the custody of your kids against the cult; making it on your own, and now turning around and suing the cult for damages. You were conned into joining the Children of God," she said seriously. "If you had known what the group was really like, you never would have joined. Never. They deceived you by withholding the true facts about themselves and 'Moses David.'" She spat out his name in disgust, "That dirty old pervert! Just because you made a mistake by joining them does not make you a failure or a misfit," she said looking at me with warm, compassionate eyes. "You made a mistake once, but that doesn't mean that you will spend the rest of your life making mistakes. You are a strong, intelligent person, even if you can't see it right now. But I have faith in you, in your abilities and in God," she said as she reached out and squeezed my hand. "And so does my family. You are very special to us and we love you."

Their faith and love was the soil from which my own feelings of self-confidence and self-worth began to grow.

The First Congregational United Church of Christ in Tallmadge, Ohio, gave Marcia the support she needed when she left the cult. Now this friendly congregation and its pastors, Rev. Arthur Arvay and Rev. Ed Carter, accepted me into their midst without judgment or condemnation. They showed me true Christian love through their actions, not just their words. Though they helped out with physical necessities, they made me feel like a worthwhile, contributing member of the church community.

"You have something to give this church," Ed Carter said one day, " . . . a wealth of experience which you can draw on to teach others. The kids in the confirmation class need to be warned about the dangers of cults—and you can tell them! If you decide you'd like to fill this special need, we'd be honored to have you speak to them."

"I'd be delighted, Ed."

"And remember, Una, Art and I are always available if you want to talk."

I smiled at the friendly, stocky man. My admiration for him had grown over the year I had been attending church. He was genuine and down-to-earth, with a vibrant concern for the congregation. His religion was not based on the emotional quicksand of cultic fanaticism. I felt it was safe to be open and forthright with him concerning my feelings about religion.

"You know, Ed, the biggest problem I have with my own faith is believing that God let me be so deceived in His name. I was terrifically sincere during my cult days . . . I really believed I was serving God . . . but obviously I was sincerely *wrong.* Why would God let that happen to me?"

"Una, do you believe that God has given us a free will?" Ed asked in reply.

"Yes."

"And do you believe that we have to take responsibility for our own choices?" he continued.

"Y . . . yes," I said slowly and thoughtfully. I began to see a paradox in my reasoning. "I believe I'm beginning to understand. It was my own decision—although an uninformed, bad decision—to join the cult. I chose—not God or anyone else. It was also my decision to leave when I did. How can I say I believe in free will and at the same time blame God for letting me join the Children of God? That is immature and irresponsible, placing the blame elsewhere. Ed, that throws a whole new light on the problem."

"So," continued Ed, "God is not to be blamed for making you do or not do anything. You made your own choices. But He was there to help you when you did decide to leave. The things that you have accomplished since you left are nothing short of miraculous."

"Nothing short of miraculous." That phrase was to haunt me for a long time. A chance long-distance phone call to a judge in London. A kind-hearted lawyer. An understanding judge. Loving, supportive friends, family, and church. A healthy mind with which to think and reason. A mighty hand working steadily and unseen to repair a broken life. Miraculous? Yes, I believe so.

Not For a Million Dollars

When the telephone rang that morning two years had passed since I left the Children of God. During that time I had struggled long and hard with my fury at Greg and it had abated. I believed he had been sincerely misguided. I blamed the influence of the cult and its mind control for his bizarre and hideous behavior. I believed that inside the "Children of God mold" there lived the real Greg, a good and honest man. But the trust between us was shattered, irreparably. In November of 1978 we dissolved what was left of our marriage.

I directed my anger at the true culprits—David Berg and the Children of God. From other ex-cult members I learned that conditions worsened after I left. Prostitution became mandatory. Orgies and bigamy were sanctioned. Child sex including pornography were introduced. VD flourished, and illegitimate babies were born every day.

My anger burned against Berg for the brainwashed adults, but even more for the innocent children. Who would protect their rights to a decent life? And how would the general public ever know the depths of Berg's depravity unless I, and others like me, exposed it?

For eighteen months, I pursued a lawsuit against the cult, charging them with breaking up my marriage with their doctrines on sex and misrepresenting their beliefs to me in their attempt to convert me. For eighteen months, a suit had been *pending against the cult, charging them for the damages to my marriage and for misrepresentation of ideals.*

"Hello, Una, this is Leda Hartwell," the familiar voice said briskly. "Things are progressing better than we could have hoped. The cult has fought every step of the way, but the judge refused to throw your case out of court. He feels that you have a very legitimate and serious complaint against the group. Could you come to Columbus on Thursday to testify in Judge Gillie's court?"

"Don't worry, Mrs. Hartwell, I'll be there," I answered.

Thursday was a sunny, sticky day near the end of June. The air on the bus was hot and stifling as Marcia and I rumbled toward Columbus. I was filled with grim determination. This was my day in court—my chance to strike a blow against the corruption of David Berg—for myself, for my children, and for other hostages of the cult.

A bevy of teenage girls sat nearby, chatting and laughing about their school outing and their boyfriends. I reflected that I was only their age when I fell into the clutches of the Children of God. How young and innocent I was then! But that all seemed to have happened an age ago, in a different world.

We found the courthouse by one o'clock and took the elevator to the fifth floor. Marcia and I walked down the long hallway. As I opened the handsome courtroom door, a little story that I'd heard once in Ireland flashed through my mind:

A weary young mother was walking down the street with her two young children when she was stopped by a wise, old man. "I'll give you a million dollars for those two fine children," said the old man. Surprised by his strange offer, the mother replied, laughingly, "Sir, not for a million dollars would I give up my children." A twinkly look crept into the old grandfather's eyes. "Ah, my dear, then you are rich indeed!"

A
Child
of
Our Time

A quarter century ago, when I was in college, young people were not much affected by religion. Secularism, materialism, and get-rich-quick ideas were dominant. Professors and social commentators in general declared that ours was a world come of age; human reason, working through science, was in control. Religion was relegated to the arena of feelings, taste, and wish fulfillment. The church seemed powerless to affect the course of world events. The parents of young people wooed by religious cults today are of my generation. It is hard for them—as it was at first for me—to understand the vastly different conditions in high schools and colleges today.

Since we (the parents) were young, the bland fifties, marked by the first overseas war against Communism in Korea, were followed by the turbulent sixties. The sixties brought not only youthful opposition to the second anti-Communist war in Asia, but also a rising interest in the religions of Asia, in native American religions, in the bizarre practices of the occult, and finally saw the rise of new religious cults in America. As the seventies wore on, these new, syncretistic, wildly heretical faiths such as the Unification Church (the Moonies), the Hare Krishna movement, the Way International, and the Children of God blossomed. These groups, still on the rise as we begin the decade of the 80's, were opportunistic responses to the feelings of lostness and the desire for authority figures on the part of the young. As Paul observed in his day, many people in our time "have a zeal for God, but not according to knowledge" (Rom. 10:2).

As these strange, exotic forms of religion settled down in America, they were accompanied by a surge of interest in a simplistic and escapist form of Christianity. The Jesus People movement spread among our youth. Churches began to grow, especially those using the method of the mass media. To the casual observer, America seemed to be thriving. Yet, as Martin Luther observed, "Where God builds a church; Satan erects a meeting house."

The simple, undisciplined forms of Christianity were not able to protect themselves from the power-seekers and fanatics in every movement. The Jesus People were taken over, in many cases, by leaders like David Berg or drawn into the Way International. Without a system of checks and balances on their activities—which can only come from a denominational structure—the charismatic leaders sometimes perverted their followers' idealism and founded anti-Christ cults. The zeal of sincere seekers was exploited.

The People's Temple of Jim Jones is a striking example. After the Jonestown massacre and the revelations of religious prostitution preached by many disciples of the Children of God, even the most devout—or most secular—person can see the point of Jesus' declaration about false prophets: "By their fruits ye shall know them" (Matt. 7:20).

The decade of the sixties may finally be classified by religious historians as the age of the occult, and the seventies as the age of cults. Some scholars have estimated that more than 5,000 religious cults, from a handful of members in size to tens of thousands of adherents, flourished in the seventies. Unlike my generation, American youth have turned to religion with a vengeance. Unfortunately, like unwary buyers in a market, many youth cannot tell the genuine expressions of religion from the false; nor can many of their parents. There is much need for factual information, for reports of real life experiences with these false faiths so that others may be forewarned and saved from unnecessary suffering.

That is why Una McManus' story is so important. She is a child of our time. She has been through the fire and has emerged to warn us of the dangers in religious fanaticism. Una has experienced the hippie subculture, the tragedy of drug abuse, the feelings of alienation from family and church, the attraction of the "love bombing" of the cults, the surrender of her liberty to the absolute power of cult leaders, degradation, exploitation, disaffection and courageous escape. *In listening to Una, we are hearing what one of the victims of Jonestown would tell us, if that were possible.*

Una's story is a model of what can happen to any of our children if we neglect their spiritual welfare. Christian parents need to know Una's story and to make it available to their teenage children. There will be far less shock to our children in reading of Una's misadventures than in being drawn into a cult themselves. Most particularly, we should point out to our children how the religious cults misuse the Bible, prayer, doctrinal beliefs, speaking in tongues and, especially, present-day hopes and fears about the return of Christ and the end of the world. *Religious fanaticism is not religious faith,* but is—as Paul called it—"another gospel: which is not another" (Gal. 1:6–7).

What causes religious fanaticism to develop? Undoubtedly, there are many causes, but these are some significant ones:

• Fanaticism, spawning a favorable climate for cults, arises in a period of great social upheaval and rapid cultural change. This kind of rapid and dislocating change has characterized America for over twenty-five years.

• Great and sudden change causes uncertainty and

fear. Fanaticism, and the desire to find unquestioned, authoritarian leaders, is an attempt to deal with fear and uncertainty on the part of some people. Psychologically, there is a defense by denial—a denial that anything has changed by the assertion of absolutes.

• Much change is moral change. Religious fanaticism often arises to denounce changes in morals and to insist on the old ways—although the fanatic may actually define as moral what ordinary Christians rightly condemn as immoral.

• Fanaticism results from misplaced idealism, especially the other-worldly idealism of Scriptural literalism, such as Millenialism. Interestingly, every religious cult, whether based on Hinduism or Christianity, from the People's Temple to the Unification Church to the Hare Krishnas to the Children of God, is millenially oriented, and specifically pre-millenial. This means that all cults announce the imminent end of the world and the final judgment in the context of great disasters and catastrophes, like the battle of Armageddon, mentioned in Revelation, chapters 19 and 20. Even the cult of the Ayatollah Khomeini in Iran is millenialistic, as it grows out of the Shi'ite sect of Islam that looks for the return of a messiah to purify the earth.

When one believes the present age is soon coming to an end and that one's final salvation is in the balance, then fanaticism, and the resulting cults, can develop. This is the illogical reasoning of Jim Jones, David Berg, and even of Charles Manson and the Ayatollah Khomeini. When we think it strange that men and women in our time can be swayed by cult leaders, we need to recall the words of the noted Swiss psychiatrist, Paul Tournier:

> Modern man despite appearances, is less aware of his own nature and motives and is lonelier as he faces them. We pity the savage amid his mysterious, menacing spirits, but at

least he shares his fears with all his tribe, and does not have to bear the awful spiritual solitude which is so striking among civilized people.

The primitive tribe does at least lay down a certain magical interpretation which, however mistaken, is satisfying because it is unquestioned. In the same way, the modern fanatic, who unhesitatingly accepts all the dialectic and the slogans of his party is happier than the skeptic. And this explains the strange resurgence of the primitive mentality which we are witnessing today.

When Una McManus tells us of her life with the Children of God (or "the Family"), we are given a rare and important experience in learning for ourselves and for our children. This is not because her story is so bizarre, but because she is so much like ourselves. We, too, have high ideals. We, too, once found, or still find, ourselves strangers and afraid in a world we never made. We, too, are besieged by voices calling for our commitment or warning of doom on every hand. The re-emergence of the Cold War because of Russian actions in Afghanistan and the turmoil in Iran in the 1980's guarantees that these voices of doom will grow louder and that our fears will become even more intense. We need guidance to tell the truths of religion from the perversions of our faith, that the New Testament warns are sure to come (See II Timothy 3:1–9; II Thessalonians 2:1–12; Colossians 1:8; Ephesians 5:3–13; Galatians 5.)

Una's experiences are precisely in accord with the information given me about cult teachings and practices by more than a dozen other ex-cult members whom I interviewed as background for this study. The first-hand witness of these now free people is that religious cults can be recognized by eight major elements:

1. A literal, pre-millenialist apocalypticism—i.e., the cults teach the literal, catastrophic end of the world soon.

2. An attack on the beliefs and teachings of all other churches, groups, and sects.

3. An aggressive, relentless proselytizing of new members, often accomplished by "love bombing" or tremendous ego-stroking.

4. A high demand for commitment for fulltime, life-long service in the group. Parents, friends, and all outside interests are to be relinquished.

5. Psychological manipulation or "brainwashing" in which control is gained over the new members' minds. Techniques of "mindbending," such as speaking in tongues, recitation of hundreds of Bible verses without regard to content, or meditation, are taught so the cultist throws his mind "out of gear."

The isolation of new members and brainwashing are sure signs of a cult's existence. Cults move on from aggressive proselytization and making high demands on their members to cutting their members off from the rest of the world by isolating the member. The cult is thereby able to control all the information that the recruit receives. This is similar to the solitary confinement of the POW's who were brainwashed during the Korean War. Now, behavior modification begins. By keeping the recruit from the influence of family and friends, and by drilling him in the teachings of the cult, he can be programmed or conditioned to parrot the cult line without thinking for himself. Isolation is one of the marks that horrifies parents, and literature is now full of cases where these parents have kidnapped their own children from communes and cult headquarters.

6. Members are subjected to personal and economic exploitation—they must give up all their possessions and solicit funds from the public.

Everyone has seen cult members out begging or soliciting funds through the sale of pamphlets, candy, etc.

Some ex-cultists have disclosed that they each have raised more than $30,000 a year. These funds are all turned over to the cults. While the cult members live under the harshest conditions, cult officials live comfortably, the top-ranking leadership often living in multi-millionaire luxury.

Exploitation can be personal, too. Jim Jones' sexual exploitation of both men and women in People's Temple is not unique. The classical cult configuration includes sexual deprivation, from the primitive witch cults to the Children of God who train young women to be "hookers for Jesus" using sex as a means of proselytizing.

7. Members are taught to be totally submissive to the cult leader. His or her word is law and is usually claimed to be the revelation of God. Some claim to be the end-time prophet or even the new messiah.

Almost without exception, cults are marked by absolute, unquestioned allegiance to one person. This can be the Maharishi, the Rev. Moon, Rev. Jones, or Victor Paul Wierwille. In many cases, the words and writings of the cultic leader are considered superior to any other religious scriptures. David Berg says it is better to read his Mo letters than to read the Bible, for the Bible was the Word of God for yesterday and his letters are the word of God for today. Wierwille claims only his method of biblical research in the Way can tell you what the Bible means. This divinization of the leader is a sure mark of a cult.

8. Members are taught to practice "heavenly deception," i.e. to misrepresent their groups, their activities, their beliefs, and their purpose in soliciting money.

This practice of deception in their dealings is used, both with their own members and with outsiders. What cult members often don't know is that they are being deceived, too. For example, the Unification Church operates under forty-eight different foundation and corporation names, most of which do not contain the term,

Unification Church. When a contribution is made, the contributor is not told to which of these groups he is giving. Also, when people are recruited, they often do not know what group they are joining. This secrecy means that only the very inner circle of cult members have any real idea of the purposes and operations of the group. Even long-time members may be completely in the dark.

Thus a cult is marked by isolation of new members, followed by conditioning or brainwashing; total loyalty to one person, who often claims to have the only religious truth; economic exploitation, both of members and outsiders, and the practice of deception about the identity, purposes, and programs of the group. Whether we condemn cults for the falseness of their teachings or not, we must condemn their practices as unchristian and undemocratic.

All of us, adults and teenagers, are subjected to the stresses, changes, and dangers of our time. We all long for security, and not unnaturally look for something solid in religion. Yet there has always been false as well as genuine religion. For every Moses bearing tablets of the law, there are others who dance around golden calves. *False religion* preys on our baser passions, our fears and desires. It asks for our freedom and promises us an elite place in God's plan in return. *True religion* asks for our faith, and gives us our freedom.

Cults, as organized expressions of false religion, are generally ruled by autocratic, self-appointed leaders who want absolute control over members. The only protection we have against attractive, charismatic religious leaders who may be tempted to become cult leaders is membership in a church body that exercises discipline and checks and balances upon the beliefs and activities of local church leaders and groups.

Early warnings that something may be wrong include the subtle and persistent proselytizing of members by "love bombing." Taking advantage of people's needs is not a Christian trait. The use of sex appeal—women used to recruit men and vice versa—is also a clue. Cult leaders can often be spotted as "Big Daddy" father figures of the incestually, sexually attractive type. Jim Jones, with his sex relations with both male and female members was not unusual. Sexual abuse is part of false religion and, historically, of cults.

Leaders and groups which spread pessimism and anxiety about "the last days" and the supposed evils of the present day are also to be examined carefully. Fears about imminent catastrophe, the end of the world and the possible loss of one's salvation are frequently used by cultists to stir up anxiety in potential recruits and to hold power over cult members. Una's story makes this clear—and the witness of every other ex-cultist interviewed—makes even clearer the fact that fears about the end of the world and the coming judgment were the most important elements in their recruitment to the cults. Amazingly, this was true of persons who entered the Hare Krishna group and the Divine Light Mission (based on Hinduism) as well as of those who entered Bible-based cults like the Children of God.

The Christian Church today must help men, women and children develop a healthy faith. While such a faith includes many things, it must at least include:

• The recognition of God's grace in Christ; that Christ has set us free from the power of sin, death, the Devil, and the law. We are not to allow anyone to lay another yoke of slavery to law or leader or "new revelation" upon us.

• The recognition that although saved, we remain all too human. Daily we must confess our sins, pray to God through Christ, and remember that we were made fellow-heirs of the Kingdom of God with Jesus Christ. As saved sinners, we are not perfect; we are justified by faith and sanctified by the blood of Christ. Cultism is generally a form of works righteousness that attempts to make people more than "mere Christians." God's Kingdom is for "mere Christians"; there are no elite inhabitants of heaven.

• The recognition that true Christianity gives us a healthy taste for freedom. We are freed in Christ to think for ourselves, to be reflective, critical, and open-minded. God is God of truth and Lord of fact. We don't need to be brainwashed, protected, or indoctrinated to be Christians. God sets our minds and spirits on a high place in Christ. We are to resist anyone who tries to tell us what to think and how to think. If we cling to our freedom of thought and belief, no cultist can deceive us. The church should promote such emotional and intellectual growth and integrity in all people.

• The recognition that social and personal ethics are paramount in true religion. We can never do ill that good might come. Only God can bring good out of evil. We are to conduct ourselves as honorable children of an all-good and merciful God who has shown us His grace in Christ.

With that grace, we need no cults or charismatic leaders.

One Christ is enough.

JOHN CHARLES COOPER

GLOSSARY OF TERMS

Agagism
the sin of disobeying a leader.

Babe
a new member in the group. New converts are treated and regarded as infants until they complete the indoctrination program.

Babe's Ranch
the indoctrination center for new recruits.

Colony
the home of two to twelve cult members, houses given to the group by new members, properties donated by businessmen, or rented apartments paid for by the money collected on the streets to help drug addicts.

Deprogramming
a system designed to bring a person out of the cultic brainwashed state and make him independent of the cult.

Family (the)
the informal name of the Children of God. The Children of God now sometimes use the name "Family of Love."

Flirty Fishing
religious prostitution. A word play on Christ's command "Follow me, and I will make you fishers of men" (Matt. 5:19).

King David
David Berg, alias "Moses David." The leader of the Children of God, who proclaims he is empowered by the spirit of the biblical King David.

Leader in training (LT)
a six-month period for new members proven loyal for six previous months, in which they are given limited leadership responsibilities under supervision. This stage opens the confidential realm of Moses David's

teachings and letters. After a year of training is completed, the leader is considered capable of starting his own colony in another city or country.

Litnessing
distributing Mo letters for a donation.

Lost sheep
a prospective member who appears receptive to the cult.

Moses David
the leader of the Children of God. He commands implicit obedience within the group, claiming to be God's greatest and last prophet on earth. Within the group he is referred to as "Dad" and "Papa Lion."

Mo Letters
pamphlets and booklets written by David Berg, alias Moses David, expounding his beliefs, interpretation of the Bible, and alleged revelations. Numbering close to a thousand, many of these Mo Letters have been bound into Bible-like volumes. Berg is still writing them and cult members consider them the inspired word of God for today, as the Bible was for yesterday, and are obeyed as such.

Mo Tapes
cassette recordings of the Moses David letters. Sometimes produced under "The Wild Wind" label.

Mo Quotes
a quote from a Moses David letter. Mo quotes are memorized and referred to in the same manner as Bible verses.

Older brother or sister
the stage of training above "the babe" level. The older brother or sister has completed the initial indoctrination process and is given limited responsibility. If he proves himself loyal and unquestioning, his responsibilities and stature within the group are increased.

Procurer or provisioner
a Family member who persuades businessmen in the

group, generally on the pretext that the Children of God help drug addicts.

Regional mother
a female leader who oversees the domestic affairs of several colonies in the same area.

Revolution (the)
The revolt of the Children of God against established Christianity.

Set-Card
a small card listing several hundred Bible verses to be memorized. These selections were chosen by David Berg to prove his interpretation and distortion of the Bible.

Shamers
members who do poorly distributing Mo letters and soliciting donations.

Shepherd
the leader and spiritual authority within a colony.

Shiners
members who excel in distributing Mo letters and soliciting donations. They are extolled as true disciples and others are encouraged to emulate them.

Systemites
people who live outside the group in the "System" or world society. They are generally regarded as damned and Devil-controlled.

Tribe reports
members' detailed reports to their leaders, including number of Mo letters and Bible chapters read, verses and quotes memorized, and personal problems encountered that day.

DATE DUE

Demco, Inc. 38-293